Can You See My Dust?

CAN YOU SEE MY DUST?

Lisa Bell-Wilson

Red Engine Press
Fort Smith, Arkansas

Copyright © 2024 Lisa Bell-Wilson

ALL RIGHTS RESERVED. No part of this book may be reproduced or transmitted in any form or by any means, electronic or mechanical, including photocopying, recording, or by any information storage and retrieval system (except by a reviewer or commentator who may quote brief passages in a printed or on-line review) without permission of the publisher.

Cover Design by Joyce Faulkner

Library of Congress Control Number: 2024930937

ISBN: 979-8-9895620-2-2 (softcover)

Dedication

For Maxine who wanted John's story to be written more than anyone else.

Table of Contents

Prologue .... *vii*
1 ♪ The Beginning *1*
2 ♪ Radio Flyer Wagon *5*
3 ♪ Can You See My Dust? *9*
4 ♪ Cherry Bomb *11*
5 ♪ Go Cart *14*
6 ♪ Ford Fairlane *16*
7 ♪ White Tail Deer *19*
8 ♪ Fishing Trip *21*
9 ♪ Parachute Club *23*
10 ♪ Entrepreneurship *25*
11 ♪ Match Made *27*
12 ♪ The Old Landlady *30*
13 ♪ The 'Rehab' *32*
14 ♪ Mowing the Lawn *35*
15 ♪ Abandoned Building *37*
16 ♪ The Abduction of Miss Unclad *52*
17 ♪ Hospital Rescue *55*
18 ♪ Dumb Pills *58*
19 ♪ Night at the Movies *60*

20 Yellow Bucket	62
21 Adventure on the Rails	64
22 Dallas-Fort Worth Airport	67
23 Washington D.C.	74
24 Near Drowning of the Crippled	77
25 Family Reunion	80
26 Art Downtown Kids	84
27 Lefty	87
28 Old Blue	89
29 Christmas with the Yankee Dog Mayor	91
30 Oh! Lovely Christmas Tree!	97
31 Cabin on the Lake	101
32 Birthday Cake Artwork	103
33 The Starship	105
34 Grandma's Pickles	107
35 Thrift Store Artwork	110
36 Avatar	113
37 The Mysterious Lady	115
38 Passing of the Torch	117
39 The Woman Behind the Man	123
Acknowledgements	125
About the Author	127

Prologue

I CAN STILL HEAR HIS VOICE in my mind. Mostly on stormy days, I can feel his presence in the room. In my mind, I see his dark hair and mustache peppered with gray, dark eyes sparkling. Most often he dressed in plaid shirts or in warm solid colors matching his skin tone. He was well spoken, with a smooth, even tone of voice. He had a way of putting people at ease. It is evident after his passing that John Bell Jr. touched many people's lives. In surmounting his obstacles, he set a standard for everyone he met that said, "Take nothing for granted. Seize every opportunity given to you with your two good hands."

John Bell Jr. was born in 1937 with a birth injury that caused cerebral palsy. The condition caused tight muscles that interfered with his ability to walk. His arms were also affected, and his hands turned under at the wrists. As a result, his appearance made him seem an unlikely person to succeed as an artist. At first glance, a person might see him only as someone confined to a wheelchair. However, there was a lot more to him than it appeared. John did not allow his limitations to define him.

John began drawing when his mother gave him pencil and paper to keep him occupied while she did chores. As a boy, he learned that he could use pencil to make an exact copy of the characters depicted in his comic books. Soon he was able to observe a real word scene and reproduce it on paper. He spent his life developing that talent.

John also had a kind heart and a fierce desire to better not only his life, but also the lives of others with disabilities. He knew what it was like to fight for every opportunity in life. In the 1970s, he was known as an activist in the Fort Smith area, working to improve access to goods and services for people with disabilities. He became a lifetime member of the Fort Smith Jaycees, was President of Arkansas Chapter of United Cerebral Palsy and was appointed to the Governor's

Commission on People with Disabilities. Of course, he was best known as an artist. His career evolved over the years from airplane model designer to fabric designer. In his later years, he developed a reputation depicting Arkansas history on canvas. His paintings are historically accurate and bring to life scenes of Fort Smith and the regional area in the early 1900s. He gave the scenes relevance by surrounding the intended subject with members of the community as they would have been in living history. His last piece was a commissioned work which he completed a couple of months before his death.

John's work as an artist defines the man he was in his professional life. This book tells the story of who he was in his private life. I am his daughter and know a side of him unfamiliar to most other people. To understand who John Bell Jr. was outside of his work, a person only needed to hear him recount the events that made up his life and appreciate the physical challenges he faced every day.

John was a master storyteller. He spoke about his experiences eloquently and spun those tales with a remarkable sense of humor. He used facial expressions, voice inflections, and his extensive vocabulary to paint verbal pictures for listeners much like his paintings recreated historical scenes for viewers. Through his stories, he touched deeply, and often changed their view of the world. This book is a compilation of his stories. Some are written in his words, and others are from the viewpoint of his friends and family. John was a husband, a brother, a father, and a grandfather. He was also a friend and hero to many. Please enjoy the stories of his life.

Lillian Sweeten Bell and John Bell Jr. 1937

1 ⚭ The Beginning

IN THE 1930s, FORT SMITH was very different from the bustling town we see today. Gender-revealing parties and birthing suites were yet to come. It was a time for midwives and house calls, particularly for families who were not well off. John Bell Jr. was born at home to parents Johnny Henry Bell and Lillian Sweeten Bell on October 4, 1937. His father worked as a carpenter. His mother was a homemaker.

The small frame house where John was born is gone now. In its place is a vacant lot near the railroad tracks. Depicted in John's painting, "After the Storm," the house stood on North Short L Street. The following is a recounting of the night John was born, based on years of hearing the story told at the family holiday table.

Lilly Bell had been scrubbing floors, washing clothes and dishes all day. Although the Bell home was modest, Lilly kept it immaculate. Her husband Johnny was 10 years her senior. He believed housework was "women's work." Lilly knew her job was to keep house and have babies. She also knew that at that moment, she was preparing to do both. Although this was her first child, she knew she was in labor.

She put away the last of the dishes and peered out of the kitchen window. Dark clouds were rolling in. The bed sheets on the clothesline flapped in the wind. Lilly grabbed her laundry basket while running out the back door. She hurried down the four wooden steps and across the lawn. Then it hit. Another labor pain made her stop her work. It seemed to last forever as she stood in the yard, hands on her knees. The wind tossed her hair. She caught sight of something blowing in the wind out of the corner of her eye. It was her laundry basket. Large drops of rain began to fall. Lilly needed to get the laundry inside without the basket. With an armload of sheets dotted with raindrops, she climbed the steps to the small front porch. Just as the door closed, rain peppered the windows of the house. Another labor pain coursed through her body. The sheets dropped to the floor. Her husband sprang from his spot on the couch.

"Darn it, Woman!" He picked up the sheets.

The tears in her eyes were enough to make him realize that the baby was on the way. The bed was made up…this time by a carpenter's calloused hands.

The vigil began. Johnny Senior smoked a pipe and walked back and forth across the living room floor. "Where in tarnation is that midwife!"

Unable to stay in bed, Lilly walked around the kitchen using the furniture and counter for support. The midwife arrived on foot, drenched to the bone. Leaving her wet coat on the porch, she went inside. Nobody would hear her knock in this storm anyway.

Johnny Bell greeted her with, "How long does it take to get here? She's about done had that baby all by herself."

The midwife did not stop to talk with him but headed straight to the bedroom to help Lilly. As an aside, she told Johnny, "Women been havin' babies by themselves since Mother Mary birthed baby Jesus. You just sit a spell and stay out of the way."

Johnny resumed pacing the floor, smoking his pipe, and monitoring the storm outside.

The midwife dressed Lilly in a loose gown. "It'll be a while before the baby arrives," she told her. "Lie down and rest now."

Lilly did not rest easily. Used to hard work and little rest, she continued to walk the floor. Alternately, she stood at the kitchen sink, bent over with pain, her black hair wet with sweat. Leaning over the sink made her appear even smaller than her already petite 4'11" stature.

The hours ticked by…and Lilly labored on. The wind blew the screen door, banging it against the house. There were no streetlights to shine on the house as darkness fell. Lilly was a strong woman, but she was getting tired. The midwife checked for progress and finally gave unsettling news. The baby did not turn during labor as was hoped. She summoned another midwife to help to turn the infant. Johnny Bell paced across the living room floor, smoking his pipe and listening to cries coming from the bedroom.

Two midwives were unable to make the baby turn. Finally, Johnny Bell summoned a doctor from downtown. They didn't have the money to pay a doctor, but the midwife explained to Johnny that there was no choice. Lilly was in trouble.

Johnny waited a long time for the doctor to arrive. Finally, he heard boots on the front porch. He opened the front door, and the doctor came in with the wind.

"Sorry, I had to go 'round," the doctor said. "The bridge washed out." In a low voice, he told Johnny that a choice had to be made here, and that it was likely that the baby was already lost.

Johnny said, "I understand. Just do what you have to do."

The doctor entered the small bedroom. The light was dim except for lightning flashes from outside. The smell of sweat and blood was thick in the little room.

The doctor helped Lilly give birth to the baby. The midwives worked to stop her bleeding. The baby was blue and not moving. The doctor tossed him on the corner of the bed and turned to wash his hands. He left the midwives to care for the two.

On his way out, he told Johnny, "I'm sorry. Your baby is dead."

Now Lilly cried…not just from pain, but also because she knew there was no cry from the baby. One midwife tended to the baby, and the other to Lilly.

They tried to comfort the young mother, saying, "It'll be all right. You can try again."

Outside, the storm was subsiding. The midwife ran a basin of cold water, and one of warm water. She picked up the infant and placed his tiny body alternately in warm water and then in cold. Finally, a baby's small cries filled the modest frame home. The sun began to rise. It was Lilly's 17th birthday.

Lilly was told that John Bell Jr. would be lucky to live six weeks. She had his picture taken so she could remember him. Lillian and John Henry Bell never imagined that John Bell Jr. would live for 76 years and become a very successful artist.

John Bell Jr. and Carolyn Bell Hughes 1942

"Carolyn didn't come to my rescue. It didn't take long for me to realize I had to save myself from drowning in two feet of water!"

2 🔔 Radio Flyer Wagon

JOHN BELL JR. GREW UP playing in an area of Fort Smith called Bailey Hill. Many 1940s' neighborhood children have fond memories of Bailey Hill. A large water reservoir dominated the top of the hill. In its hallmark days, the Hill also boasted a swimming pool and a playground. According to John Bell's stories, a lady coordinated lots of activities for the children including games and swimming. This is one of John's stories about being a Bailey Hill kid.

JOHN BELL:

One sticky hot summer, my sister Carolyn and I were home and bored out of our minds. You could see heat waves rising from the road. We decided to go to the park and swim. Back then I didn't have a wheelchair. I crawled everywhere I went. I wore suspenders to keep myself from coming out of my clothes. The park was about four blocks from our house, and it was uphill. It would take me forever to crawl there.

We decided to use our radio flyer wagon. The idea was for me to get in, and for Carolyn to pull the wagon to the park. Our house had four wooden steps, but no ramp. I told Carolyn to back the wagon up next to the steps. I crawled out on the porch and scooted sideways until I was lined up at the edge of the porch. Then I rolled off the porch and onto the top step, and down one more step. Then I scooted toward the right edge of the step, headfirst, toward the wagon below. The whole time, Carolyn was telling me, "No, Junior! This isn't going to work. You're gonna get hurt."

"It'll work," I said. "I've done this lots of times."

Of course, I slid into the wagon headfirst, and scraped the side of my face. I told Carolyn I was fine, never mind the stream of blood running down my face onto my shirt. She helped me get upright in the wagon.

Carolyn pulled the wagon…and talked. It was steaming hot. At about the halfway place, she pulled the wagon over under a tree to cool off. I sat in the wagon, and she sat under the tree…and talked. We started back toward the park, and finally I saw the pool on the horizon. It looked like a mirage, and I wondered if it was real. I was so hot I thought I could already feel that cool pool water! Carolyn pulled the wagon up to the shallow end. Since the pool was sloped on the bottom, I could sit in the shallow end and not get in water over my head. I sat there, listening to her talk and talk.

The water felt so good and so cool that I almost drifted off to sleep. Then I felt the ground shake as a huge kid ran past. I heard his wet feet going "splat, splat, splat" on the concrete. Just in time, I saw him hurl his big fat body off the side to jump in the water. Too late, I yelled, "Nooooo!" I knew he would create a pool tsunami that would be the end of me.

Next came the huge wave. I took a great big breath and was washed down the slope of the pool into water that was over my head. It didn't have to be very deep to be over my head. At first, I thought, "Carolyn is right there, she'll see and come pull me up."

Carolyn didn't come to my rescue. It didn't take long for me to realize I had to save myself from drowning in two feet of water.

"John, don't panic," I told muself. "If you panic, you're a goner."

I thought about the bottom of the pool and scoped out which way the slope went. I was an expert at rolling, so I rolled up the slope of the pool, and rolled and rolled…finally I was up by the wall of the pool and got my head out of the water. I was gasping for air and pool water was all in my nose. Finally, I got my breathing all evened out. Then I heard Carolyn. She was still sitting there talking. She never realized that I almost drowned.

Going home from the pool was easier because it was a downhill trip. What we failed to realize is that a radio flyer wagon loaded with one crippled boy can gain speed going downhill. Carolyn was walking, trying to hold back the weight of the wagon by pushing on the tongue. She walked faster and faster. Then she was running and trying not to get run over by the wagon with me in it.

She finally stopped talking and screamed, "Junior! Junior!"
I yelled, "Jump in!"

Carolyn jumped in the front of the wagon, crushing my legs under her weight. The wagon rolled faster and faster downhill, weighed down by one girl and one crippled boy. We hit rocks and bounced up and down, side to side We both screamed. I tried to get hold of the tongue of the wagon to steer it. Finally, we were near the house. In front of our house was a big, deep, dirt ditch. The wagon hit a rock, veered to the left, and we landed at the bottom of the ditch with the wagon on top of us.

Carolyn yelled, "Junior! Junior! Are you okay?"

"Yeah," I said. "I'm okay. Just get the wagon up out of the ditch before Mother comes out and sees us."

We were both bruised up and had road rash on our sides. My face was already scraped from earlier. We looked terrible.

I crawled to the shallow end of the ditch to get out of it. Then I rolled uphill and out of the ditch. Of course, I was wet with pool water and blood, so I was a mess. I crawled across the yard and started up the four wooden steps to the porch. By then, Mother was on the porch yelling, "Junior! What in the world happened to you?" I was covered with mud and blood.

I just said, "Nothing. I'm okay."

That night, Carolyn and I started working on a plan to make brakes for that wagon.

John Bell Jr. and brother Jim Bell 1950

"I loved to get in the road on my board and go as fast as I could! I thought I was flying!"

3 🔔 Can You See My Dust?

AS A YOUNG BOY, JOHNNY Bell Jr. wanted to be like any other boy his age. He enjoyed playing with the other kids and roamed the neighborhood with them as much as he could. When he was a teenager, a local charity organization provided him with a wheelchair. He never forgot what it was like to be a small boy having to crawl everywhere. This is his story about what that meant to him.

JOHN BELL:

When I was a boy, my parents never got me a wheelchair. A friend's dad noticed me crawling everywhere. They lived a couple of blocks away, and I often ended up in their yard, playing with the other boys.

One day, he said, "You're that Bell boy?"

I wasn't used to being called into conversation by another boy's dad, and I wasn't sure if this was a good thing.

"Yes, sir."

"How did you get all the way over here? Your folks bring you?"

"No, sir."

Well, it was obvious how I got there. The only way I could get anywhere was to crawl. I noticed him watching me, so I figured it must be time to get back before he got onto me for something.

A few days later, I was out on the street in front of the house. Now, the street was dirt. That meant when it rained, it turned to mud. The cars drove through the mud and made huge ruts. When I was a boy and crawling everywhere, those ruts were so big I almost got lost in them. I would get in one and crawl until I got out of it on the other end. I looked to my left and saw a dirt wall. I looked to my right and saw another dirt wall. I liked to see how fast I could crawl through a rut from one end to the other, like a car might go.

One day, I was crawling in a rut and here came a car. I heard it and imagined that I felt the ground rumble. I looked behind me, and here came a huge car tire. I panicked. I knew I was about to be run over. I put in high crawl gear! The car rolled slowly behind me. When I got to a spot where I could get out of the rut I turned sideways and rolled over and over until I was in the grass in someone's yard. I imagined I had just avoided being squashed to death.

Then the car stopped, and the door opened. A man got out and opened the back door. I knew I was in trouble for playing in the road, so I tried to hightail it across the yard. I didn't even know or care whose yard it was.

Then I heard the man's voice say, "Johnny Bell?"

I knew I was busted for sure. I stopped in mid-crawl. The man caught up to me, which wasn't hard to do. He had something in his arms. I saw that it was my friend's dad who had been watching me way over in his yard. He knelt and put the thing on the ground.

"I made something for you," he said.

Well, nobody ever made anything for me, so I didn't know what to say. I looked at it, not sure what it was. "Thank you, Sir," I managed to say.

"Why don't you try it out?"

He had made a board with wheels under it. This was a little like a skateboard, but with only one set of wheels. I could get on it, stomach down, and crawl with it under me. The wheel rolled and the board kept much of my body off the ground. If I balanced just right, I could propel myself with my feet, balance on the wheels, and go really fast!

Once I had that board, the road was a whole new thing. I loved to get in the road on my board and go as fast as I could. I thought I was flying like Superman. I went as fast and as far as I could, and then I would look back to see how much dust I was making fly up. It was a lot of fun for a crippled boy.

4 🔔 Cherry Bomb

BUILT IN 1928, FORT SMITH High School (eventually named Northside) was a two-story building that was not wheelchair accessible. FSHS was the only high school in Fort Smith until 1963, when Southside High School was built. Access for the handicapped was not a priority in those days. John Bell Jr. went to FSHS until he graduated in 1957. While there, John navigated the architectural barriers presented by the old building through his own ingenuity. This is his story about his High School adventures.

John Bell Jr. Senior Picture 1957

JOHN BELL:
    Even though there were stairs and no elevator, I had to attend classes just like the other students. I had to figure out a way to get up

the stairs, so I made friends with guys on the football team. Those boys were big enough to carry me upstairs. Back then, I had a manual wheelchair that was easy to fold up. How this worked was, one guy carried my wheelchair upstairs, and another guy put me over his shoulder and carried me up. Then they put me in my wheelchair so I could go to class. The perk for this service was that the guys who carried me got to leave class ten minutes early. I really couldn't afford to make any enemies because I needed all the friends, I could get…and I knew everybody.

There was not a lot of mischief going on at school during those days, mostly people skipping class or smoking in the bathroom. Sometimes bullies would beat up someone. However, there was never anything like what happened the day of the cherry bomb.

It was just a regular Tuesday. I was hanging out in the hall waiting for a ride home. It was almost summer break, and it was scorching hot outside. Back then they used big fans in the halls because the high school wasn't air-conditioned. It was late, and the school day had been over a long time ago. I sat there in my wheelchair, listening to the fans running, waiting.

It was so quiet in the halls that I almost nodded off. Suddenly the back door to the school slammed open. A guy popped his head in, leaned inside and threw something that bounced down the hall, hit the wall, and rolled under my wheelchair.

The guy in the doorway yelled, "Oh my Goodness! Bell! RUN!"

Well, I couldn't run…I reached down and caught hold of the wheels on my chair. I got in one, maybe two shoves on the wheels…

Then all the sudden, "BOOOOOOMMMM!" Something exploded. The hall filled with smoke.

I couldn't hear anything but a high pitched, "EEEEEEEEEEE!"

The door to the office popped open. I saw people running toward me. I didn't think I would ever be able to hear again.

The next day there was an inquisition about the whole thing. The principal called all the likely suspects into his office and questioned each person, one at a time. He called me in first. I felt small sitting in my wheelchair on the other side of his giant oak desk. I already knew what this was about.

The principal said, "Johnny, who did this? Now, nobody is in trouble here, we just want to know who it was."

He was lying. I knew that someone's head would roll…just like that cherry bomb. There was a black spot on the floor that wouldn't mop up, and more than one of the lockers was all black and dented. I could barely hear. I thought about all of that. I thought about the guy I saw in the doorway tossing the cherry bomb.

Then I said, "I don't know who it was. I didn't see anything but smoke."

The principal stood up, leaned over his big desk and looked down at me. "Now, think about it really hard. Are you sure you didn't see anyone?"

"No," I said, "I just heard an explosion. Then there was all this smoke. I swear!"

I did know who it was. The principal knew that I knew who it was. The boy who did it knew that I knew. But nobody could prove anything. And I wasn't talking.

5 ⚏ Go Cart

JOHN BELL:
BACK IN HIGH SCHOOL, SOME of the boys I hung out with were a little rough around the edges. They had cars and could drive, and I had a job and some money. I worked for Berkley Models, drawing model airplane plans. They would pick me up, put me in the car and my wheelchair in the trunk. And then we went riding around. Mostly we drank beer and pop and played pinball games. One night, they decided we should go to the go-cart track. Well, they had drunk a lot of beer. We got to the go-cart track…and they all rented go carts. The only way I could ride one was to sit in it with someone else who could work the gas and the brake.

  They put me in a go-cart with Joe. He got in, and I sat in front of him. We started riding around and around the track. They were all trying to see how fast they could go. We started going faster and faster. I hung for dear life. I watched the curve come up over and over again. The go-cart fishtailed around the curve and then straightened out. Then Joe started trying to run the others off the track. I hung on, my eyes as big as saucers. Then he swerved into another go cart, hit the curve, and slid into the wall. The go-cart turned on its side, and Joe slammed into me, pushing me forward. My chest hit the steering wheel and my leg jammed into the floor of the go-cart. Everyone came toward the cart and set it upright.

  Those boys pulled me out of the go-cart and got me back to my wheelchair. I told them my leg was hurt. They said they would put me in the car and take me home. We all got in the car, but they decided they wanted to ride around some more. I told them to take me home. Eventually they did but by then, my leg was swollen badly. It was late, and I didn't want my old man to know about my leg or how late I came in. I got in bed and lay there with my leg hurting until Mom got up.

Turned out my leg was broken. I spent forever in a cast. I couldn't get in and out of bed or do anything on my own with that thing on my leg. After that, I decided I better find a way to get my own danged car.

Johnny Bell Jr. with first painting sold 1957

6 ♿ Ford Fairlane

JOHN FINALLY DID GET A car. Back in that day, there were no cars built with hand controls for handicapped people. John figured out how to make them for his car. He drew some plans, and had a friend make and install them. There were no hand control tests, or test dummies, only John. He later designed a prototype of a van to be used by a person in a wheelchair. He was a risk-taker. If he had not been, nothing extraordinary would have ever happened in his life. He wanted control of his own life with the freedom to come and go as he pleased. The ability to possibly kill himself seeking this freedom was a risk he was willing to take.

JOHN BELL:

When I was in high school, I worked part-time for Berkley Models, drawing airplane model plans. I saved up enough money to buy a used car off a buddy of mine. It was a 1954 Ford Fairlane. I designed a system for hand controls using some metal rods, and had a friend fix it up so I could drive it. Back then, I could get in the car, fold up my wheelchair and pull it into the back seat.

When I first got the car, I had a hard time finding someone to teach me to drive it. Lots of people were willing to drive me around in it, or borrow it, but nobody wanted to teach me to drive. One night, I went with a buddy of mine to the naval reserves where he had a meeting. While I waited outside in the parking lot for him to come out of the meeting, I decided to do some practice driving. I eased the car out of the parking lot onto Wheeler Avenue, then out to Towson to a little drive-in. A carhop I knew came out to take my order. I visited with her and bought a soda pop, like I had always wanted to do. It was great. Some of my other friends pulled in, and we visited for about an hour. I drove the car safely back to the naval reserves building to pick up my friend.

When I got back to the Naval Reserve Center, the parking lot was empty. The meeting had ended early, and practically everyone in Fort Smith was out looking for me.

I loved having a vehicle so I could go out and do all the things that my friends did. I hid it from the Old Man because I didn't want to hear him tell me how I shouldn't be driving. We lived on North Short L Street, off of Towson Avenue. One day, I decided to go ride around. I got in the car and started her up, put her in gear and rolled down the dirt alleyway toward Towson Avenue. I thought I was rolling a little too fast, so I took off the gas and pulled the hand control to hit the brake. Nothing happened. I went faster and faster and there was nowhere for me to turn off and nowhere to go. I could see cars swishing past on Towson! I tried to make an escape plan. I hit the intersection moving fast, pumping that brake and picturing myself slamming into someone.

I thought, "Bell, how are you gonna get out of this one?"

By the grace of God, I didn't hit anyone. There was a gas station on the other side of Towson Avenue. As I watched, it got closer and closer. As I sped across Towson, I saw two guys out front working on a car. One was almost upside down inside the engine compartment and the other stood beside it looking at the engine. They both glanced up as I barreled onto the station lot. They looked back at the car, and then looked up again. When they saw that I wasn't stopping or slowing down, they yelled and scattered into the station. I grabbed the wheel and turned the car away from the building. Somehow, I managed to swerve around the gas pumps and not hit one while picturing a flaming explosion that didn't happen!

After that, I jerked the wheel and swerved back out onto Towson Avenue. I was steadily thinking of an escape plan. A few blocks down the road, my sister Carolyn and her husband, Jimmy, lived in an old house with a steep alleyway in the back. I knew if I hit that alleyway and headed uphill, the incline would slow the car down. I also figured Jimmy would come to help me out. I saw that alley coming up and jerked the wheel. When I hit the dirt in the alley, the car skidded a little sideways, plowing up dirt and gravel. It jerked me sideways, and I slid on the car seat down where I couldn't reach the wheel anymore! I was down in the seat, praying the car would come to a stop. I heard yelling and screaming. Looking up through the car window, I saw the top of Jimmy's head, bobbing up and down as he ran alongside the car.

He was yelling, "Johnny! Johnny!"

Jimmy grabbed the door handle and got the door open, slung himself in and jammed on the brake pedal. The car slid to a stop, rocking back and forth so much I thought it was gonna roll. Carolyn caught up to the whole scene with Jimmy still standing on the brake, the door open, me laying on the bench seat and dirt flying all around.

Carolyn yelled, "Johnny you're gonna get yourself killed!"

After all of that, I decided I better get a brake job.

LISA BELL-WILSON:

John said, "Later, I heard from Jimmy that he and Carolyn were sitting out on their back porch smoking. They saw a crazy person careening onto the alleyway driving way too fast.

"Carolyn yelled, 'Look at that crazy fool!'

Jimmy looked, and said, "'Dang it, Carolyn! That's Johnny!'"

7 🔔 White Tail Deer

THE STATE OF ARKANSAS BOASTS some of the most beautiful, wooded countryside in the nation. Rolling hills covered in towering pine trees that shadow hiking and biking trails make up the Natural State. There is nothing like the peacefulness and tranquility you feel in the middle of the Ouachita or the Ozark mountains. The sounds of the breeze blowing through the trees and birds singing is music to the soul.

Unless you happen to be in the "Deer Woods." Then things get serious. The very snap of a twig is deafening. It could be the crack of a shotgun and smell of gunpowder. It might be the thought of bringing home enough meat to fill a freezer. Whatever it is that drives men, young and old, to hunt deer in the woods must be inherent to being born a boy in the first place. John Bell's dad went hunting. His friends went hunting. He wanted to go hunting too. Of course, it's almost impossible to actually go hunting if you need to use a wheelchair to get around. John's dad never took him hunting. But his friend Harry Elledge took him. Somehow, they both lived to talk about it. This is John's accounting of his hunting trip.

JOHN BELL:

Harry and I decided to hunt some whitetail one day. My old man went hunting all the time, and I wanted to go, but he never took me. So, Harry picked me up in his pink Nash Rambler, threw me in the front seat and the wheelchair in the trunk.

We took off and he said, "Okay, John, I found a good spot in the woods for you. Here's what we'll do. I'm gonna go off and scare out some deer. When they come running out, you shoot 'em!"

I was trying to picture how this was going to go. Harry pulled off the side of the road and got my wheelchair out of the trunk. He came around and handed me two big shotguns, picked me up and put me over his shoulder. Harry was walking through the woods, and I was hanging over his shoulder with these guns, and I started thinking, "I wonder if these things are loaded?"

We got to the spot and Harry sat me in my wheelchair. So, I was in the middle of the woods in my wheelchair with this big shotgun. Quite a sight for sure.

Harry said, "Okay, I'm going way over this way. I'm gonna flush out some deer. When you see them come running, SHOOT!"

Harry went off crashing through the bushes. I sat there and I waited. I waited and I heard birds. I waited and I heard squirrels. Then I started hearing something else. I wasn't sure what it was, but I was thinking it might be a deer! I saw something moving in the woods, but I couldn't tell how far away it was. So, I situated myself where I was pointed toward the thing. I put my elbow up on the arm of the wheelchair, finger on the trigger of the big shotgun. And then I waited. I started to hear voices.

I was thinking, "Oh No! That's not a deer!" Then what came out in front of me but my Old Man!

He saw me in the woods in my wheelchair with that big gun.

He was with one of his buddies, and they were three sheets to the wind with shotguns in their hands.

I lowered my shotgun.

The Old Man said, "What the tarnation are you doing out here, Junior?"

"I'm hunting," I said. "What in the tarnation do you think I'm doing?"

8 🔔 Fishing Trip

JOHN AND HARRY ELLEDGE WENT fishing from time to time. He told this story about a fishing trip he would never forget.

JOHN BELL:

Harry carried me over his shoulder to the bank of the river. He helped me get situated, sitting on the ground with my back against a tree, fishing line in the water. I was all set. Harry was fishing up and down the bank. Pretty soon, I couldn't see him anymore. Well, it was a hot summer day. A breeze was blowing. So, I drifted off to sleep. After a bit I thought I felt something that might be a tug in the line. I opened my eyes. I looked down and saw this huge tarantula crawling up my leg! I was so scared I could barely speak.

I was afraid to move, so I started saying, "Harry! Harry!" The thing was getting up near my ear.

"Harry! Harry!" My voice came out like a little squeak. I couldn't make any sound.

Harry finally came running, but he couldn't see the tarantula behind my head.

I squeaked out, "Spider!"

Harry said, "John, I don't see anything!"

Then he saw it and yelled, "Oh Crap!" and started beating me and the tarantula with his fishing pole. I'm not sure who came out the worst, me, or the tarantula.

In Harry's telling of this, he said, "Well I was off fishing on the bank of the river. I started hearing a woman's voice screaming something.

I was thinking, "What's a woman doing out here in the woods and what is she screaming about?"

Then I realized it was Johnny screaming.

John Bell Jr. in art class at University of Arkansas
1957 with an unknown student

"He was a risk taker. If he had not been, nothing extraordinary would have ever happened in his life."

9 🔔 Parachute Club

JOHN BELL HAD AN AMAZING sense of humor. It was his sense of humor and his desire to be a part of everything everyone else was involved in that sometimes got him in trouble. When it came to John and his friend Harry Elledge, it was hard to tell which one of them was the ringleader. This is Harry's story about John's membership of the University of Arkansas Parachute Club.

HARRY ELLEDGE:
    While we were at the University of Arkansas, I had a sport parachute club. We took people up and let them parachute down into a field. I was trying to get Johnny to be able to jump. I would take a tire and put a small parachute on it and throw it out of the plane, but the chute wouldn't open.
    When I explained this to John, he said, "Well it would probably open for me. Let me try it."
    "No, John," I said, "…this might turn out to be more of a problem than we expect. I can take you up, but I need to be sure I can also get you back down." John was game with anything because he wanted to be a part of everything.
    Later on, a couple of Razorback ball players called me wanting to jump. They said, "We hear that you have a parachute club, and you can take us up."
    I said, "Yeah I do, but you'll have to get through some training first."
    They came on over and I put them through ground school. At the time, I was dating this busty girl named Brenda. She was a really big girl. I got her involved with getting those boys ready to jump. I also got John involved. I put Brenda out there, and she acted like she was going to jump, too. Everyone was putting on vests.

Brenda threw her hands back and said, "Can one of you help me with this strap?"

You could NOT get that strap fastened. It was impossible. One of the Razorbacks tried to help her. He was breaking out in a sweat the whole time.

John sat over by the airplane in his wheelchair while I was taking those Razorbacks through ground school.

I would turn around to go to the plane, and John would say, "I want to go up! I want to go up!"

"Shut up! You know you can't jump anymore." I didn't break a smile.

Johnny said, "No, I want to go up!"

"Shut up!"

This went on for a while.

Then the guys looked at me and said, "What happened to him?"

I didn't answer them. Johnny was having a fit, acting like he was mad that he couldn't go up. He flailed his arms around, making noises and saying how he wanted to go up.

Finally, the Razorbacks said, "NO. You have to tell us what happened to him."

"Okay," I said. "He was the president of our club a couple of years ago. The chute didn't open and that's all that's left of him."

"Oh, my Goodness," they said. You could see the macho draining out of their faces.

10 ♭ Entrepreneurship

ONE OF JOHN BELL JR.'s friends while growing up on Baily Hill was Perry Grizzle. They became lifelong friends too. Perry told about the unextinguishable entrepreneur that John Bell Jr. was. This is his story.

PERRY GRIZZLE:

When we went to the University, we were poor. I mean really, we didn't have much to eat. John decided he was going to do something about that so we wouldn't have to worry about groceries anymore. He designed a good-looking razorback hog license plate. This was before the days when lots of hog merchandise was available. There were some Razorback memorabilia, but his razorback looked different than anything out there. We sent it off and had it made up. Those plates came in boxes of 500, each separated by paper.

When game day came, we took the boxes and a card table and set up on the parking lot at the University. We sat John at the table with a metal box to put the money in, and he drew up a sign to advertise the plates. We paid fifty cents for each one and sold them for five dollars.

We all unboxed the plates, took the paper off, and handed plates to the customer. John took the money. We had a good thing going. Then we looked up and saw two men coming toward us with name badges on.

I said, "John, I bet we are about to get shut down." We knew we didn't have permission to sell those things.

"You boys go over there and watch,"John said. "They won't shut down a cripple."

So, we went over to the side and acted like we didn't know who John was or what was going on. We watched as those men came over and started talking to him. Next thing we knew, they were taking out the plates, separating the paper and handing the plates to the customer. John put them to work!

We made a lot of money on those plates. We split it up and had groceries for a long time.

John and Maxine Bell
at University of Arkansas Student Union
with fellow students

11 ♁ Match Made

IT WAS OBVIOUS THAT JOHN Bell Jr. and Maxine Tincher were made for each other. Maxine had contracted polio at the age of seven, along with her brother, Charles. She recovered but was unable to walk and used a wheelchair. This fact gave her something in common with John Bell Jr. and she admired him from afar.

Maxine's face lit up every time she talked about meeting John. They first met while both were in grade school. Maxine's family soon moved to Charleston, and they parted ways for a while.

This is her story about how they met again.

MAXINE TINCHER:

"The school at Charleston wasn't handicapped accessible, so they sent teachers out to the house to teach me at home. I hated not being able to leave the house or play with other children. Then one of the teachers recommended that I go to school at the Joseph M. Hill School for Retarded Children." In those days, children with handicaps were often treated as though they also had intellectual disabilities, even if that was not the case.

"I had been taught at home for a long time, and I was afraid to go to a school where I didn't know anyone. When I got there, I was excited and surprised to see Johnny again! He helped me get to know the other students and helped me with some of my assignments."

LISA BELL-WILSON:

The two parted ways again when John went to school at Ramsey Junior High. A long time passed before Maxine saw him once again, but she never forgot him.

Maxine's mother, Lucille Tincher, ran an eatery in Fort Smith called the 'Highway 71 Café.' The Café was a destination for Johnny and his friends to play pinball machines. The story was that the machines actually paid money if you won. This is Maxine's story about their reunion:

MAXINE TINCHER:

"My brother, Charles, worked at the café. One day Johnny came in with a bunch of his friends. Charles spotted him and showed him a picture of me. He asked Johnny, "Do you remember this girl?"

Johnny said, "Of course, I know her!" Charles set it up for me and Johnny to meet at the Café. We met and began dating."

John's friend, Harry Elledge, of course, was one of the first people Johnny introduced to Maxine. Harry told me all about the day he met her. Here is his story.

HARRY ELLEDGE:

Back in the day, John and I did a lot of running around. One day he came up and said, "Harry I want to take you out to the café."

I said, "What for?"

"You'll see."

Johnny and I drove to the Café on Hwy 71. I got him out of the car and put him in his wheelchair. We walked into the café and there was this girl in the booth with a wheelchair beside her.

Johnny said, "Look at that, isn't she pretty?"

I said, "What are you looking at?"

"That gal sitting over there."

"Yes, she's a pretty good-looking gal."

"I like her a lot," he said.

So, I said, "Bell, look. When we go places, I'm carrying you. If you pick this girl up, that means I carry her too. If I carry both of you, I have to have a wheelchair in each hand. Can't you get somebody that walks?"

He said, "No, I like HER."

"So, the rest was history."

Maxine Tincher Bell Class Picture 1953

12 ⚲ The Old Landlady

THIS CAN'T BE THE PLACE. I was thinking that, as I stood in the street looking up at a parking deck. It was hard to believe that the search for the places my parents had lived in led me to this spot. In the 1960s, Lindell Street was on the edge of the University of Arkansas campus in Fayetteville. The apartment John Bell Jr, and Maxine lived in is gone now, but some of the old rock houses, rose bushes and wisteria still stand on neighboring blocks. John and Maxine lived there while attending college. While standing on the spot that marked their address, I looked north, uphill. Then I looked south, also uphill. Remembering John's stories that I had heard all my life about Lindell Street, the details began to make sense. I heard his words in my head as though they floated on the late Spring breeze.

JOHN BELL:

At the University of Arkansas, we lived in an old apartment on Lindell Street. The apartment was barely accessible to wheelchairs. The sidewalk out front was broken up, and it was uphill to the campus no matter which way you went. It's hard to push a wheelchair uphill. This was a four-plex building, and Perry Grizzle and Harry Elledge lived upstairs. The old lady who owned the place was a first-class bitty. There was something about me she just didn't like, and she made no bones about letting me know that every time we talked. We had this old, beat-up dining table, and all the furniture we had was old. One time, the apartment next door was vacant. From the open door, I heard banging and scraping, vacuuming and furniture moving. I saw through the door that the apartment had lots better furniture than the furniture we had in ours. I asked the old lady if we could switch the furniture while that place was empty.

She said, "No! That furniture stays in that apartment."

"Why? The place is empty. It would be easy to switch the furniture before someone else moves in."

"No, Johnny, you don't pay enough rent to use that furniture."

That made me mad. The apartments were the same size, so I figured the only reason she didn't want me to have the furniture was because she didn't like me. I talked to Perry…and we came up with a plan. In the middle of the night, Perry and some guys broke in there and switched the furniture. They also put about a thousand booze bottles everywhere in the vacant apartment. They hid bottles in the toilet tank, in all the cabinets, and everywhere else. Then they closed the place and locked the door.

Not long after that we were making dinner, when I heard the old bitty next-door yelling, "Johnny Bell! Johnny Bell!" She came over and banged on our door. "You got that furniture. You took that furniture when I told you to leave it alone."

"What are you talking about?" I said, "Now how do you think I took that furniture? I can't move furniture. I thought you had changed your mind. I came home, and the furniture was switched so I thought you had done it."

"No," she said, "I know you did it. I know you did it."

"Now how in the world would I do that? I can't even get into that apartment."

She knew I had something to do with it, she just didn't know how I did it.

Later she started finding the booze bottles. She would find some bottles and yell, "Johnny Bell! Johnny Bell!" Then she would come and bang on my door, and say, "You come get these bottles!"

I would say, "What bottles? You know I can't get in that apartment."

She hauled out sacks and sacks of bottles. Only she didn't find all of them at once. Later she found more. She thought I had gone in and hidden more bottles.

She came over and yelled, "Johnny Bell! Johnny Bell!" There we went again.

It was all worth it because we finally had the better furniture.

13 ⚕ The 'Rehab'

TOWERING ABOVE BATHHOUSE ROW in downtown Hot Springs is a huge building originally constructed as the Army Navy Hospital. Built in 1887, it was one-of-a-kind. At the height of World War II, it served more than 95,000 soldiers. In 1960, the building was turned over to the State of Arkansas and became a rehabilitation hospital operated by Arkansas Rehabilitation Services. The facility offered restorative medical services and vocational training to people with disabilities. In 1965, John Bell Jr. had all but completed a degree in art and education from the University of Arkansas. He needed to satisfy the practice teaching portion of his degree, but no school in Arkansas would allow him in to teach because he used a wheelchair. It was widely held that he would be unable to control a classroom while sitting in a wheelchair. So, he taught art at the Hot Springs Rehabilitation Center to complete his degree. He had many stories about "The Rehab."

As the adult child of two people with disabilities who used wheelchairs, I became a Rehabilitation Counselor and began working for Arkansas Rehabilitation Services in 2005. After a day of meetings at "the Rehab," I had some time to walk the halls of the giant building and reflect on its history. Bright rays of sunshine lit up the hallway on the 6th floor of the main building where I stood thinking about the stacks of ceramic molds in the arts and crafts area. It appeared that not much had changed in many years, and I wondered if those same molds were there during the time when John Bell Jr. taught art in that very room. I remembered his story about teaching there. This is John Bell Jr's story about his time at "The Rehab."

JOHN BELL:

I was a teacher at the Rehab, but I looked like a student. Many students in attendance at the Rehab had physical disabilities and used electric wheelchairs like mine. During my first week there, I was required to complete the whole semester's worth of lesson plans to be approved by my advisor. I stayed in the dormitory with the rest of the students. This saved me from having to pay for an extra place to stay, but it was a mixed bag. I was up late every night that first week. I had to teach all day, and then work on my assignments for my classes at night. Back then, the Rehab students had a curfew. Lights out was at 10. The night housing staff monitored who was following the rules. On Monday morning, I was called in on the carpet.

"Mr. Bell, there is a problem," was what my Rehab Center advisor said.

"What problem?"

"You were up too late at night, all week long."

I couldn't believe this. "Up too late?"

"Yes, the night watchman turned you in. You were up past midnight every night last week."

"What? Of course, I was up late. I teach all day and do my schoolwork at night. I'm not a student of the Rehab, and I shouldn't be subject to those rules!"

"Well, I understand," he said, "…but if you get turned in again, I'll have to report this to your faculty supervisor."

"You go ahead and report it," I said, not believing what I was hearing.

I went ahead and called my faculty advisor and gave him a head's up so he wouldn't be surprised when he got the call.

I told him, "Just get ready to hear about this, because I can't do all of my teaching and get my schoolwork done before 10:00."

I was not very popular among the staff there at the Rehab from the beginning. Aside from breaking curfew, I also noticed that the food they served to the students was not the same food that was served in the middle of the week when the faculty was there. We had good food until the weekend, and then it was all cold cut sandwiches. Since I was a student, and a sort of faculty member, I was asked to speak at the Rehabilitation Services Advisory Council meeting about how it was to be there at the Rehab. The Council served as an advisory board to

Arkansas Rehabilitation Services. I told them that 'The Rehab' was a good place to get some solid vocational training.

I also let them know that there was a giant double standard there. The staff members sat at the 'staff table' and talked down to the students. On the weekends, students were fed cold sandwiches and not allowed into their 'bank accounts' to draw out money if they needed anything. It turned out my choice to sit among the students instead of at the 'staff table' was just as well. I wasn't welcome at the staff table anyway.

When I graduated, I wrote up some recommendations for the Rehabilitation Council on how to improve conditions for the students at "The Rehab." I wasn't sure if they took any of my recommendations into consideration, but I had to stand up for those students. Nobody else was going to do it.

The building was closed as the Arkansas Career Training Institute in 2019 due to increasing operating costs and shrinking budgets. It still stands majestically over downtown Hot Springs. I would love to walk through the halls one more time. I would listen to see if the walls still echo the history of soldiers being transported to the operating room. I would also listen for the echo of a young John Bell Jr, full of fire, roaming the halls in an old Everest and Jennings wheelchair.

14 ◊ Mowing the Lawn

WHEN JOHN BELL JR. GRADUATED from the University of Arkansas with a degree, he had no idea how difficult it would be to get a job. John had a wife and a baby, and no way to support his family. His sister Lillian Bell Kropp and her family took him in for a time after graduation while he was looking for a job and a place to live. His wife and daughter lived with Maxine's aunt. Bill Kropp II was John's brother-in-law and friend for more than 50 years. This is one of Bill's stories about that time.

BILL KROPP:

John graduated from the University of Arkansas with a degree in Art and Education in 1965. It was no easy feat for him to get that degree in the first place. In addition to all the trials everyone has while getting a bachelor's degree, John had to also deal with the fact that the school was not handicapped accessible. After he finally graduated, we helped him start looking for a job. Lill helped him write a resume, and we sent those darned things out all over the nation for teaching jobs. If he got any interviews, they wouldn't hire him after they found out he was in a wheelchair. He couldn't even get a job in Fort Smith, where they knew him and knew his reputation. John was depressed because he wasn't getting any interviews, and he had to provide for a wife and baby.

John slept all day and was up all night. He wasn't getting anywhere. Lill went in and found him asleep one morning…and on his easel was a dark, foreboding self-portrait. The portrait made him look like death itself. He was truly at the very end of the road. It was so terrible that she told me that I needed to talk to him.

I sat down with John and tried to talk some sense into him. I said, "When you paint something, you always sell it. Why don't you just start painting?"

He really wanted to get a teaching job and did not concede that option yet.

I told him, "Well, if you're not getting a job and you're not painting either, you can't just sit here all the time and not help out. You need to do something to contribute. If you're not going to paint, why don't you get out there and mow the lawn for goodness' sake?"

The next day when I came home from work, John was out there in the yard with the lawn mower. He had Lill tie a rope to the handle of the thing, and he was out there in his wheelchair dragging the mower around, mowing the yard.

My ranking in the neighborhood went down several notches after the neighbors saw all of that.

15 🔔 Abandoned Building

WHILE LIVING WITH HIS SISTER and brother-in-law's family, John Bell Jr. was still reaching for independence. The ability to come and go as you please, to have your own space, were things he wanted that most of us take for granted. This story is about his adventure while just trying to get out for a bit is in his words. John's family encouraged him for years to write his story, and this is the only one he put down on paper. This is largely unchanged from his original words. The location of the building in this story is the site where the Central Mall is located now. John described that area as being an abandoned warehouse with a lake behind it.

JOHN BELL:

It had been many years since I was on the floor. As a child, I crawled, rolled, and leaped over the floor and the grass outside, exploring my world on all fours not just my yard, but for several blocks every day. I had to wear suspenders or coveralls to keep from crawling out of my pants! Even though my hands and knees were scarred and tough from crawling all day, it was good exercise, and I was stronger than if I had been doing push-ups.

But that was over twenty years ago. Now I found myself lying on a cold, hard cement floor in an abandoned building where no one would look for me. At one time this building was a saloon called "Lakeside" that sat back about 50 yards from the highway near a pond that they referred to as "The Lake." This was an area that once was the outskirts of town where people would go to meet friends and party away from downtown. On Friday and Saturday nights, the parking lot would be full. It would be vibrant, with the sounds of people as they greeted each other on their way into this relatively small place. It would be crowded!

Not now. Not for a long time. I lay on the floor watching the smoke rise from my cigarette and listening to the breeze banging a metal sign against the wall. The setting sun shone through the vertical cracks in the wall, making stark patterns like wavering jail bars in the smoke.

I said out loud, "What the heck am I doing here?" I didn't expect an answer and I didn't get one.

It was 1965. I had graduated from the University of Arkansas with a bachelor's degree and had high expectations to become an art instructor for the local school system. I wanted to support my wife and newborn daughter, to become a respected addition to the community. A reasonable goal, I thought. However, when school was out, and I had no prospects for work, there was no place to go. My parents had made it clear that we were not welcome at their place. They thought I was an invalid, and as such, had no possibility of becoming a useful member of society. They were determined that I would not be a burden to them. So was I!

Having a newborn daughter meant Maxine and I felt the need to be together more than ever. I felt the responsibility of fatherhood, the need to be there and the need to provide for my family. I desperately needed to find work. My goal throughout my college career was to become the best High School art instructor in the system. I was naive and thought that all I had to do to accomplish that was to be qualified. I would be in for a brutal surprise. My rationale was that my best chances for employment would be in my hometown where I knew everyone in the system. I found out that, even though I was qualified, I would have to wait for someone to retire or die. That meant that I had to find employment after college and a place to stay very quickly since our rent was due and our support from United Cerebral Palsy and Arkansas Rehabilitation Services would end by my graduation.

Maxine and I agreed to live separately for a short time and stay with our immediate families while I looked for work and a place to stay. She had stayed with an aunt in Fayetteville before we were married, but now there was an extra mouth to feed. We were hesitant to ask. Her Aunt said it would be all right, and her uncle was afraid to argue with her aunt.

He said to me privately, "It shouldn't take long, should it? I've got three kids here already, and it takes both of us to keep it going."

I told him, "I appreciate the sacrifice," I said, "I don't like being separated from my family any longer than I have to. It's embarrassing for me to have to do it this way, but I don't see any other choice. I'm grateful for your help." I said, "I'll be as quick as possible."

I could have said the same thing to my sister's family, whom I had gone to stay with in Fort Smith. They had answered my call for help after graduation when I asked for a temporary shelter. They had two small children, and it wasn't easy for them either, but they made room for me and tried to make me feel at home. They gave me my own room and helped me get it set up as a studio so I could paint and try to bring in some commissions. I made applications to the school systems as an art instructor. I knew that it would take time but wanted to be on the list.

I thought my good reputation as an artist in school and afterwards would make me welcome in the school system since the superintendent and other officials were the same and knew me from school. I was dead wrong! Meanwhile I applied as a substitute. I was hoping to get my foot in the door and get some class experience. I did random paintings to stay busy and portraits of the Kropp's friend's children. This was a most smothering task for an artist who just came from a university setting. Every detail was scrutinized. The nose was wrong, the chin was a little off, something about the...? A parade of little smiling faces that had to be rendered photographically.

The lack of creativity and the overwhelming knowledge that I was getting nowhere living in someone else's house, intercepting their lifestyle and not being there for my family was getting to me. I couldn't sleep. It was about 11:00 on one of those nights when I looked around the room and found myself staring back at me from a dark windowpane. My face was barely lit on one side and disappeared into the darkness on the other. There was no artificial cheesy smile, just good old honest, deep dark depression. A perfect study! Hours later, the image in the window began to fade with the morning light and emerged dramatically before me, on canvas in the dark contrasting colors. It was not flattering! I felt somewhat better, as if I had just been relieved of a week's long constipation. At last, I fell asleep and slept well until my sister woke me a few hours later. Seeing the painting, she said, "Things are not that bad!"

Even though I had only a few hours of sleep, I crawled out of bed feeling more refreshed than I had in some time. We visited over breakfast that morning while the kids were still asleep, and my brother-in-law had gone to work. She tried to convince me that things would get better, that something would be available eventually.

"Just hang in there!" She said, "You know you're welcome to stay here until you find something. You know that don't you?"

I was assured that was true and I was certainly grateful, but the reality was that I was struggling in my mind.

"Besides, if it comes to it, you could always apply for public assistance. No one could say you weren't qualified. Look at all those people on welfare that don't want to work, don't try to work, and they get rent, food…"

There it was! The dreaded description of absolute FAILURE. WELFARE was staring me in the face. These things were bearing in my mind that afternoon when I decided to go out for a while. I wanted to give them some space—to give me some space. I had a new charge on the batteries in my wheelchair; I wondered how far would they go? I would find out!

It was mid-afternoon and a nice day when I made my way to Rogers Avenue with the all-out purpose of going all the way downtown. In those days, there were not many sidewalks, which meant I had to travel mostly in the street. That wouldn't work on Rogers Avenue; it was the main thoroughfare and Arkansas State Highway 22 through town. It was well-travelled. The shoulder on the side of the road was wide enough, however, so I turned west with my eyes toward downtown Garrison Avenue. It looked like a long way. "If I make it there, I might not get back," I reminded myself as I continued along the rough shoulder in that direction, noting that the shoulder was broken in places, making it difficult to travel by wheelchair.

Although there was less traffic in 1965 than there is today, I was aware of the nearness as the cars sped by me. They offered an occasional wave and sometimes a honk and warning to get off the road.

Even though I was on the shoulder (I thought I was well out of the way), I looked up and saw a semi-trailer coming down the hill and suddenly had doubts about the safety margin. I was off the road, but the truck was big and getting bigger! It took up all its lane and a little more! Luckily, I had just found a side road when it roared by. I had gotten over far enough to feel only the wind as it passed. I was relieved at having made it but frustrated at the fact that no matter how fast you needed to go, the wheelchair moved at the same maddening slow speed. Oh well, it had gotten me to this paved side road with no traffic at the moment.

"Now what?" I said to myself when I spotted a small neighborhood bar sitting by the road a little more than a block away. It looked inviting, as bars are prone to do, so I decided to check it out. As I arrived near the parking area though, I could see two steps up into the entrance. It may as well have been a brick wall!

"Oh well, I probably couldn't get into the bathroom either. If you take a drink, you'll darned for sure have to use a bathroom." I muttered to myself as I prepared to pass by.

Then I heard, "Johnny Bell! What the in the heck! I didn't know you lived in this neighborhood!" It was an old friend from high school I had not seen in a lifetime.

"I don't live in this neighborhood. I was just passing by," I said.

No! NO! You don't just pass by a perfectly good beer joint. Hey Sam!" He yelled into the bar, "Come on out here and help me haul John's tail up these steps."

"What for? We'll just have to haul it back down again." Another old friend stood at the door wearing a big grin and holding a can of beer.

"Sam! I'll be darned!" I said, shocked to see them both.

"No doubt about that," He said as he took charge of one side of the chair and they both lifted me up the steps and into the building.

I lingered there for a short time over one beer, talking more than drinking, trying to recover a sense of myself by connecting with the past. I felt better after a while, but also felt another need slowly building. I decided to check out the bathroom before it became serious. The doors to the bathroom stalls were too narrow! Now it was serious.

I made excuses to my friends and headed down the road thinking my only choice would likely be back at the house, but I preferred something closer. Looking around for anything to hide behind, I spotted an abandoned building about 50 yards off the highway. It was a stone building with a large window smashed by vandals, glass scattered everywhere. It looked good to me.

I rolled up to the doorway and looked in. The door was lying on the floor at an odd angle across the room. It was resting in layers of broken glass that covered the long rectangular room. Here and there, whisky bottles lay, also broken. Shattered glass was a silent witness to the occasional visitor. A 10-foot-long oval opening, once a window, looked out on the barren parking lot and the passing cars beyond. With no glass in the windows, the traffic sounded closer than it was. I felt too exposed in that room, so I looked toward a small back room that might have been the original restroom and storage. Whatever it was, that was the place.

Looking it over carefully, I saw it was about 12 feet square with a cement floor that was about 4 or 5 inches lower than the adjacent room. It was surrounded by a wooden wall made of vertical boards that you could see between. It was a shed. Not pretty, but private enough for my needs. I was concerned about the drop down to the next level. Afraid I might not be able to climb back out of it, I looked around among the debris and found a board the right size to form a small step down that would make it easier to climb back out.

"Plan ahead…" I said out loud to myself, as I scooted the board into place with my foot and then rolled down into the room to the nearest corner. That's when I realized another moment would have been too long!

Then, I sat for a little while to enjoy the quiet, and prepare myself for the journey back, hoping that my engineering effort would allow me to climb back up on the way out. This is what was on my mind when I turned around as I backed up and felt my left back wheel go down in a shallow ditch!

"Oh Dang! Now what?" I said out loud. No one answered.

This was a cement floor except for one indentation about a foot wide and two inches deep that ran across the room. I have no idea why it was there or what it contained before, but now what it contained was me! A sense of urgency crept over me. No one knew where I was, nor would they likely look for me here. "If I'm to get out of this place," I thought, It's up to me to do it. Unless one of those drunks looking for a shelter stumble in here, I'm on my own."

It was getting late, not long before dark. It was most important that I drive out of here through that room full of glass. I struggled trying everything I could to get the one side of my chair that was in the ditch to crawl up at angles out onto the cement, but the more I tried, the deeper it sank into the dirt. My chances for escape were getting dimmer along with the light that streaked through the wall behind me, casting long shadows that looked like jail bars.

I knew there was only one thing that would work. The only thing to do was to get to the floor and lift the front wheel out of the ditch. I had to do that in order to turn the chair sideways and allow the back wheel to roll up onto the floor. I could do that. The trick would be to get back up in the chair from the floor. I wasn't so sure about that.

I yelled out one more time as the next car passed. I knew I was too far for anyone to hear me. I took my cigarettes out of my pocket, threw them on the floor along with my wallet, then carefully eased myself down to the floor. It was very hard and painful to my bare elbows as I rested on my right side and pulled myself along with all my weight on my right elbow. I knew that, since I was left-handed, I could then use my left hand to raise the wheel out of the ditch. With no weight in the chair, it was easier than I thought and soon I had it out of the ditch and up against the wall where it wouldn't move as I pushed and pulled my way back up into it.

I thought to myself, "That's the plan, now it's do or die!"

I lay on my back, taking a short break, put my cigarette butt in the ditch and rolled over on my side, resting on one elbow, a bare elbow that told me how hard the cement was. I thought, "It has been years since I had to do this!" So long that I had to think about the mechanics of moving about on the floor…crawling!

It was not as simple as it sounds. Instead of placing both hands and knees on the ground to see which one out-knee could the other, I had to scoot along on my side. Propping myself up with one elbow, I pushed with my legs, leaned forward, and pulled with the elbow which propelled me forward about six inches a scoot. I wasn't overly concerned about wind resistance.

My legs were permanently crossed in what was referred to as a "scissor lock," which would not allow the independent movement of my legs necessary to crawl on hands and knees, so I compensated with the push-and-pull method as described. It was much slower, wearing on the pants and painful to the elbows. I remembered as a child I was much more limber and could move about quite well by placing my hands on the ground, drawing my knees beneath me, and then springing forward like a frog (I imagined that I was flying like Superman). I was somewhat older now and couldn't fly anymore, so I made my way back to the chair the hard way, determined to get back up in it. Otherwise, it was a very long way to the highway. This fact stayed with me as I tried to analyze the problem of getting into the chair from the floor.

The chair had a sling seat made of canvas and covered with Naugahyde which was attached to the frame on either side but was loose in the middle. This was satisfactory if you transferred from an even surface (from bed to chair), the seat would stay down, but from the floor up, unless you could hold the seat down with one hand as you lifted your bottom up even with the seat, it would tend to rise with you. I didn't have the dexterity to hold the seat down, so that was my fate.

I struggled and strained for a very long time to raise up higher than the seat, but as I pulled up, the seat would hang on my belt and go up with me. I could see that the struggle was not gaining me anything. I was exhausted and wasting time. I had to save something for the next big struggle.

Now there was only one way out! I made my way back to the same spot on the floor and told myself I would lie there for the duration of one smoke, then I'm leaving. I must have help to get into the chair, and the only way to get it is to make it to the highway. The only way to get there is to crawl, scoot, whatever it takes. I mulled over this problem, smoking my last and listening to lonesome sounds of a distant dog bark, the loose tin sign banging and a faraway passing car.

"All right. Let's get on with it!" I said to myself.

I raised up on one elbow and scooted over to the edge of the door to the next room. The floor of the next room was slightly higher. I rested my elbow on the board that I had placed there earlier and peered into the darkness at the glistening broken shards of glass covering the room.

I thought to myself, "If I get out of here without bleeding to death, no one will believe me, and if I don't, it won't matter."

That was it. My greatest fear was being cut by a very sharp piece of glass without knowing it and bleeding out before I could reach the highway.

Darkness began to take over the room, surrounding everything in gloom. I could not see. I reached out and raked the floor in front of me. The surface was rough, but I didn't feel any pain, didn't appear to be cut, so I reached out as far as I could and swept the floor with my hand. I slowly and carefully moved forward, sweeping the floor and moving forward over and over again, stopping occasionally to feel my elbows to make sure I wasn't bleeding. I wasn't.

"If I keep this up, I might just stay ahead of that smoke!" I talked to myself to break the silence and relieve the tension. "What's that up the road ahead?" Then I saw it. As my eyes adjusted to the waning light, I made out the shape of a door. A solid wood paned door lay on the floor just a few feet away! It was about three feet wide by almost seven feet long. It lay on top of the glass, evidently knocked down after all the windows had been shattered since there was no glass on the door.

I thought, "If I can make it to the door, I might be able to scoot it around and aim it toward the doorway to the outside world and to crawl across it out of the glass." It looked like it would reach halfway across the room.

"Brillant plan, Bell," I told myself, "Now all you have to do is to make it work. That door is heavy, and you are no Hercules."

"All right!" I answered myself, "Don't get personal!"

My choices were next to none, so I had to make it work. I was determined that my daughter was not going to grow up without a Daddy.

I thought to myself, "Good, bad, and otherwise, I'm going to be there… I've got to be there. I've got to prove to those sorry jerks out there that we can make it work, we've got to make it work!"

I made myself mad enough that by the time I made it to the door, I was able to maneuver it over the broken glass, which acted almost like ball bearings, and aim it toward the outside.

It reached only halfway across the room.

"Well, that's farther than what I thought it would be!"

I crawled up on the door and checked myself for blood. I was all right. Lying on the door and looking out across the shimmering glass, I felt as though I was on a raft crossing the river to nowhere. Then I spotted a nearby board about four feet wide and seven feet long. There was another one about the same size just out of reach. I slid the one I could reach alongside the door as I moved and used it to move the other. Now I have two. I slid them alongside the door as I moved toward the end of it. There were about eight feet of glass shards between me and the outside world. After that, I would have to cross about 50 yards of imbedded gravel to get to the highway.

"HELP!" I yelled as the next car passed and continued down the road. I felt stupid, but there was no one around to notice. I wish there had been.

I continued to move the boards along until I reached the end of the door, then I laid them side by side at the end of the door and pointed to the outside world. Together they would be about eight feet across which would keep some of my butt from being sliced as well as provide a more comfortable surface for elbows. This worked well, although they fell about three feet short of the doorway. Luckily there was less broken glass at this point, so I was able to make it the rest of the way into some tall grass just outside of the building. I breathed a sigh of relief having made it through with no major damage.

I lay there for a few minutes to catch my breath and to thank God for getting me this far. Then I raised up on one elbow to see over the weeds and rolled over into a ditch! Weeds had hidden it from me while I was trying to see through them to the parking lot. I lay flat on my back looking up at the stars. I thought some very bad thoughts for a while.

Then I started to laugh. I remembered the story of the farmer who had gotten off of his tractor to help a calf out of a ditch. The farmer slipped and fell, twisted his ankle and tumbled into the ditch. He fell hard on a rock and broke his arm. As he struggled to get up, the tractor that had been left idling rolled forward and down into the ditch on top of him! Just when he thought things couldn't get worse, it started to rain!

He couldn't get free of the tractor and the ditch was beginning to fill up with water when he yelled out, "Why me, Lord? I give to the church, the Salvation Army, I support my mother-in-law, the girl scouts-etc., etc.--!"

"Why Me?"

The rain stopped. The clouds rolled back, and a booming voice said, "There is something about you that I just don't like."

I lay on my back, looking up at the starry night and laughed.

I managed to crawl up out of the ditch and onto the gravel-packed parking lot, headed for the highway at a painful and laborious crawl. By now I had decided that calling out would do no good. The only way to get attention would be to be visible at the edge of the road. But I was getting so tired and sore that I began to doubt my ability to get there. I had to stop for a minute and lie on my back while I rested and pondered the problem. I closed my eyes and listened as the traffic passed without even slowing down.

"It shouldn't be this hard to get there," I was thinking, "I'm not going to make it like this…at least not before daylight."

I was very tired…nearly exhausted…when I decided to stop for a while, to rest and consider my options. This was too slow and tiring. There had to be another way.

I tried to remember, "What did I do when I was a kid?"

Oh, yeah--- When I was a kid, we lived on North Short L Street. It was called Short L because the street was only a block long. I explored the entire block by different methods on my hands and knees or, when I was in a hurry, I would lie on my side and roll over and over till I got there.

Could I still do that?

I lay on my side parallel to the street and began to turn over, feeling very stiff, but made it all the way over on my stomach, side, shoulders, feeling every lump push into me as I turned over and over. Slowly but steadily, I could hear the traffic growing louder. No one stopped. I continued until I was just a few yards off the highway. I stopped, lay on my back, and waved my arms in the air to get the attention of passing motorists. I waved at every car that passed, hoping that some sane person would stop and at least ask if they could do something, but they continued to pass. Occasionally one would slow, then speed up without saying anything. I was getting frustrated and angry to the point that I thought if I shouted obscenities in the air, someone might at least call the police.

A car pulled into the lot not far from me and sat there with its lights trained on me and said nothing. I called out that I needed help! He said nothing again.

Another car pulled up across the street and called out to person in the first car, "What do you think is wrong with him?"

The first car rolled down his window just far enough that I couldn't reach in and kill him "I don't know," he admitted, "but I called the police, and they should be here any minute."

I felt a sudden mixture of emotion—first relief that help was on the way, second, anger that no one spoke directly to me so that I could explain that all I needed was help to get back up in my chair, that there was no need for the police. I certainly didn't want any publicity that might come with the report of the event. Exhausted, embarrassed, and somewhat relieved with the knowledge that I had been discovered, I laid back and waited, but not for long.

Very shortly, I heard a third car pull in and stop behind the second car across the street. Without hesitation, two young men got out, came directly over and helped me to sit up!

"Hey, buddy, you all right?"

"Yeah, yeah I'm all right. I just fell out of my chair and couldn't get back up in it."

I decided to go with that story instead of the truth because it would be easier for them to believe, and it was a quicker explanation. I was anxious to get back in my chair and leave before the police arrived.

"Where is the chair?" The guy looked around in the dark and in the glare of the headlights.

I said, "It's in that building. If you can go in and bring it out to me, I'll be much better. I just need to sit up and rest a minute."

One guy took off for the chair while the other stayed with me, holding me up in a sitting position.

"My Goodness man, you crawled all the way from there?"

"Well yeah," I said. "It took a while."

"I can see that!" He said, "How did you get here, anyway?"

I explained that I was staying with my sister and her family about a half mile away and I had gone out for a walk.

"How do you drive that thing? I never seen one like it!"

"You just push that button on the hand control in the direction you want to go.

"Never mind," he said, "I'll take you in there and you can drive it out. By the way," he said, "here is your wallet. I found it on the floor. You hang onto it while I get you back to your chair."

I was somewhat smaller then. He picked me up without much difficulty and all three of us headed back in while the others watched from the safety of their cars. The last place I wanted to go was back into that building, but at the same time, I was anxious to get back to comfort of my chair and in control. I planned to get in and try to get out of there before the police arrived and I had to answer embarrassing questions from people who had no concept of the problem.

The guy carried me back into the room of glass shards asking, "How the heck did you get through here without getting cut?"

He walked across the door that I had scooted around as a bridge over broken glass. We entered the back room where the chair was still sitting where I had left it, what seemed like two days ago. The one guy flashed a small light around the room as I was being carried, and then on the chair. "There you go, Fred, looks like he's got a stick shift; he should be able to peel out!"

"I bet he's ready for that," he said as he put me down in the chair. "Just in time, too. You're starting to get heavy. I don't see how you made it that far. Are you sure you're alright?" He shined the light over me.

"Oh yes, I'm fine thanks to you guys. I'm just tired and ready to get home."

I made my way outside as quickly as I could while I thanked them for their help and assured them that I would be okay. The sirens were getting louder as they approached. I looked into the darkness. I could see the first curiosity seekers were still safely closed in their cars waiting patiently for the next turn of events. I was embarrassed at having gotten myself in this situation and wanted badly to escape into the night and avoid the uncomfortable questions that were sure to come. Yeah, well, that didn't happen. I was thinking I would make my escape, only to be confronted by two patrol cars, seven curiosity seekers and an ambulance. Really, an ambulance?

In the distance, I could hear that the sirens were getting louder. The first two cars were still there, in the same place waiting. More sirens. I started out across the lot and was suddenly surrounded by two patrol cars, an ambulance, and a dozen chasers. All I could see were black shapes and headlights. The glare made an unreal landscape of dark shapes that melted and reformed as they passed between the lights and stood before me as two policemen blocking my path.

Lisa Bell-Wilson with the family golf cart 1969

"I yelled, 'Help! Help!'
I knew they were surprised to see a golf cart,
much less one with people in it."

16 ♙ The Abduction of Miss Unclad

THE FIRST JOHN BELL JR. Art Studio I remember was in an unassuming brick building on North 'B' Street. Dad called the business "The Artist's Workshop." The building included a few offices, a gallery area and some storage in the back. Dad's office included a space built up about three feet from the floor with access by a wheelchair ramp. Below the raised space were his built-in flat files. The walls on both sides of his drawing table held multiple shelves for his stereo system, phone, books, and supplies. The wall space behind his drawing table was a big white space covered by a luxurious looking oil painting of a nude lady. The lady lay on a fancy couch with plush curtains behind her. The colors in the painting were as rich as the chocolate shakes Dad and I bought from the nearby Dairy Queen. I spent my tender early years viewing the painting of this lady. Until one tragic day when she was stolen, along with Dad's stereo system and some photography equipment. The absence of the lady left a big, blank white wall.

"Dad?" I asked, "Why would someone steal your painting?"

"Subject matter," was his answer.

The whole idea that someone would break a window and come in and steal my dad's stuff was infuriating to me. The image of the reposed woman was etched in my 7-year-old brain. I knew for a fact that I would recognize that painting if I ever saw it again.

That was 49 years ago.

In the Summer of 2021, my family worked to clear out the last of the boxes from the garage of the house that was the John and Maxine Bell home on the north side of Fort Smith. The house had sold and needed to be emptied quickly. We were almost finished when I found a stack of old boxes in the corner. They were covered in dust and spider webs. It was a hot Arkansas August, and I was covered with sweat and who knows what else, and ready to make the two-hour drive home. Whatever was in that box was going to the trash bin. While carrying the boxes, I felt something shift in the bottom one. I laid it down in the middle of the garage floor, sat on an empty paint can, and opened it. Inside with the dust were some old papers and a couple of boxes of old slides. I thought surely the slides had been in the garage for 30 years, exposed to the heat and humidity. I figured they would be useless. Nonetheless, I opened one of the boxes and took out a slide. Holding the slide up in front of the fluorescent light, I squinted to see the image.

There she was! After all these years, I was looking at a picture of the nude painting, stolen from Dad's Studio. In disbelief, I sat back on the paint can thinking about how close I came to throwing the whole box in the trash can.

My husband scanned the slide to the photos on my phone, and I posted the picture on Facebook. Immediately, I got a message from my old classmate Clifton Culpepper. Clifton and I attended Northside High School together. Clifton had contacted me a few times in the past year, saying he had a story about Dad that he wanted to tell me. This day his message was urgent saying, "The story I've been wanting to tell you is about that nude painting, the one you posted on Facebook!"

I rang his phone.

The story Clifton had to tell detailed his memory of the old John Bell Jr. Art Studio which was located at the old Fort Smith Art Center on 6th street. The space used to be a carriage house and was converted to an art studio which Dad called "The Palette." In that studio, Dad sold paintings and paint supplies and taught art lessons.

Clifton said, "I used to live not far from your dad's studio, and I walked past his door every week while taking art classes at the Art Center. I was about seven years old and was too afraid to just walk up to your dad's door. I was curious though. I would look in as I walked by, and I could see him painting. As time went by, I got closer and closer to his doorway. Finally, I had my foot almost in the door…and he said, "Well, why don't you come in?"

I went in, and he was working on that big nude painting. He had a Folger's coffee can, full of paint brushes on his table. He said,

"Get a pallet brush out of that can." Well, I was seven years old, and I didn't know what a pallet brush was. I pulled something out of the can, and he said, "No, not that one." Finally, I pulled out the right tool. He showed me his pallet and said, "Do you know what color burnt umber is?" I did not know what color that was. He showed me how to get paint on the brush, how to hold it, and how to make strokes with the brush the right way to spread the paint. He let me put some paint on that painting! Now first when I looked at that painting it was just a picture of a nude lady. After I got to paint part of the painting, the nude lady transformed into art. The painting became a work of art to me, and the whole world of art changed for me. He had introduced me to the world of artwork. It was something I will never forget."

    Clifton's story about Dad gave me chills. Hearing him tell the story, I could see the Folgers can. I could see the painting. I could smell the turpentine. Although the painting of the lady is still missing, the slide and this story has brought her back to life.

17 ⚜ Hospital Rescue

WE MUST HAVE BEEN QUITE a spectacle rolling down the street as a family. Since we had no car, Mother and Dad used their wheelchairs alone to get around town. Often, I could be seen sitting on a lap, heading down to the grocery store. Born in 1965, the only child to two people who used wheelchairs, it was expected by many that I also would have some disability. I was born with crossed eyes. That condition was just the luck of the draw, and not a result of anything passed down by my parents. When I turned three, I was admitted to Sparks Hospital for corrective eye surgery. I stayed in the hospital for about three days with bandages on my eyes. Mother spent the days with me, reading and playing games to keep me entertained.

At that time, Dad worked from his first art studio called "The Palette." Located on the grounds of the Fort Smith Art Center, the Art Center was housed in the historic Vaughn-Schaap house on North 6th street. His studio was in the old carriage house in the back. When he finished work, dad came to the hospital. This is his story about the night he stayed over with me.

JOHN BELL:

I was there with Lisa all night, and I thought I could just sit in my wheelchair and nap a little in the night. When it got late, I started to seriously nod off. I looked up at the clock and saw midnight, then 1:00 AM. I decided I had to get some sleep. The room was dark except for the light coming from under the door, and the light filtering through the one inch opening of the bathroom door. I looked over at Lisa sleeping, all curled up near the very top of the bed. I surveyed the vast expanse of empty bed below her.

I thought, "I bet I can just lean over on that bed and get a little sleep."

I moved my chair close to the end of the bed. I was able to stand and lean over on the bed. When I leaned over, the bed started to slooooowly roll away from me. I felt my body sliding against the edge of the bed. I thought "Oh no, I'm going to fall on the floor!" I couldn't pull my body away from the bed again and stand up. The bed rolled and I scooted, and the bed rolled.

Then something miraculous happened. The edge of the metal bed frame caught my belt buckle and the bed stopped rolling. I was hung there in a precarious position, not on the bed, not able to stand up again. I didn't want to wake up Lisa because she couldn't help me, and I thought she would be afraid. I looked around the room in the dark trying to find anything I could use to get someone's attention from the hallway. I noticed a small slice of light coming from under the door. Every now and then, the light flickered as people went by in the hallway.

When that happened, I whispered as loud as I could whisper, "Heeellllp!!!" The feet went on by. I did this several times. Finally, I saw feet, whispered, "Heellp!" and the feet stopped.

They were joined by other feet. Then both sets of feet went away. Momentarily, someone opened the door.

This little, tiny nurse came in, took one look at me, and exclaimed, "Oh No!" in a little tiny voice.

She went back out and came in again with the biggest, scariest looking man I ever saw. He was wearing all white and had bulging muscles. Before I knew what was going on, this man wrapped one giant arm around me and sat me back in the chair without skipping a beat. At the same time, someone rolled in a recliner. That man picked me up. My life flashed before my eyes.

I thought, "Oh no, here goes!"

But he gently sat me in the recliner and then disappeared out the door. The nurse covered me with a blanket, and next thing I knew the room was empty again. Later I thought I had dreamed up the big, huge man. All that commotion and Lisa never woke up.

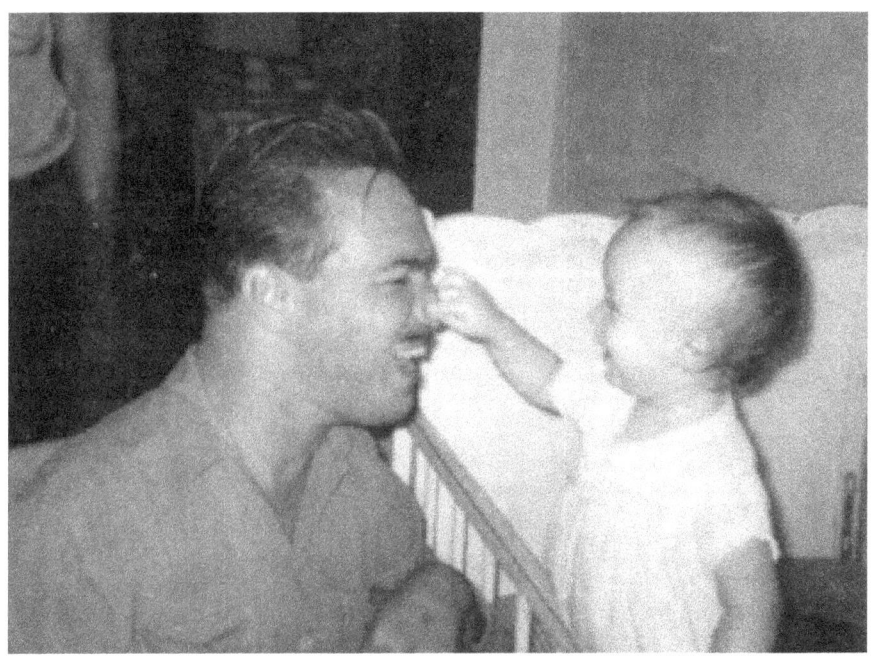

John Bell Jr. and Lisa Jean Bell Wilson 1968

18 🔔 Dumb Pills

THE EARLY 1970s WERE a simpler time. We didn't have cell phones, internet, or Facebook. It was especially simple for the John Bell Jr. family. The small house we lived in was near a grocery store and a laundry mat. Since we had no car, this was a good situation.

I was Daddy's girl. As a small child, some of my fondest memories were made when I got to go with Daddy for a walk. A walk, for us, meant Dad drove his wheelchair along the street and I walked beside him. I knew the rules were, if Mommy was cooking dinner, we needed to stay out of the kitchen.

One evening near Christmas, I remember going for a walk with Daddy. He found me and said, "Your Mother is cooking dinner. Let's go for a walk."

Excited, I put my coat on and followed him out the door. He headed down the driveway with me following behind.

At the end of the drive, he asked, "Which way are we going?"

I picked a direction, and off we went down the side of the street. Sidewalks were few in our neighborhood, but the traffic was light so that didn't matter. Examining neighbor's lawns on the way, we talked and sang songs as we walked.

We were several blocks from home when Dad said, "I took some dumb pills, so you'll have to tell me how to get back home."

"What?" I asked in disbelief. "You don't know the way?"

"No." He said, "I took dumb pills. Which way do you think we need to turn?"

I hadn't been paying attention. I had no idea which way to go so I just picked a way.

He asked, "Are you sure?"

"No. Why did you take dumb pills?" I was worried.

We turned. It was getting dark, and the houses and yards all looked the same to me.

Dad started singing, "There's a hole in the bottom of the sea! A hole! A hole! A hole in the bottom of the sea!" I joined in.

At the stop sign, Dad said, "Which way?"

I picked a way. We walked, sang, and I picked the way. Finally, I picked, and Dad said, "Why don't we go this way instead?"

"Are the dumb pills wearing off?"

He said, "Maybe. I'm not sure."

I was relieved. Finally, I saw a familiar house and I knew we were almost home. We had gone in a giant circle and ended up coming to the back of the house instead of the front.

"Daddy! There's our house!"

"Is it?" he asked.

John Bell Jr. and Lisa Bell-Wilson 1969

"Your dumb pills haven't worn off yet," I said.

"No, I guess not." He turned into the yard and headed up the ramp into the house.

Inside, I took off my coat and ran around him toward the kitchen. "Mommy! Mommy! Daddy took dumb pills. But we made it home anyway."

Next time we went for a walk, I paid more attention in case Daddy took dumb pills again.

19 ♤ Night at the Movies

THE THING ABOUT BEING A person who used a wheelchair in the 1970s is that there were no vans with wheelchair lifts. The John and Maxine Bell family owned a golf cart instead of a car. They could slide into the cart and leave their wheelchairs at the house. It was in this grand style that our family went to the drive-in movie when I was little. Dad told this story of our trip to the movies that was ill-fated.

JOHN BELL:
"Since we were slower than all the other cars, we went to the movie early and afterwards stayed until all of the other people were gone. We watched the show and ate popcorn and hot dogs. When the movie was over, I watched the last taillights leaving the drive-in. I turned the key to start the car, and nothing happened. I turned the key again and nothing. There were no cell phones or bag phones then. We just had to wait to be discovered. We all got in the floor of the cart and pulled off the cushion to the bench seat to look at the batteries underneath. We couldn't find anything obviously wrong. I resigned myself to the fact that we might be there all night. Even though it was Spring, it got pretty cool when the sun went down. I remembered the plastic "windows" that snapped on the sides. Those were tucked away where we could never reach them in the trunk in the back.

I thought to myself, "I wonder if Lisa can get into that trunk and pull out those plastic windows?" Although she was only about four years old, I thought it was worth a try.

LISA BELL WILSON:
Although I was small, I remember that night. I tried to reach the little trunk lid by standing behind the golf cart, but I was too short. When I tried to stand on the back bumper of the cart, I couldn't keep my balance and pull up the lid at the same time. So, Dad told me just to

come on and get back in the cart with them. There was one plastic window under the bench seat of the car. We all got on the floor and raised up the bench seat and Mom pulled out the plastic window. Dad's story continues:

JOHN BELL:

It was a miserable night. I lay on the bench seat of the car and Lisa and Maxine lay on the floor. I covered up with the plastic window like it was a blanket. I laid there all night staring out. Popcorn buckets and candy wrappers blew across the dirt parking lot. Dirt blew across the parking lot and into the car. The plastic window 'blanket' flapped in the breeze. A long time passed, and the moon rose. I heard a dog barking a long way away.

Somewhere I drifted off to sleep. Then a sound woke me up. I looked up and right into the face of a hound dog! The dog scared me, and I scared the dog. It backed up and stood about ten feet from the cart and barked and barked at us. There was nothing I could do to make it go away.

When the sun was barely up, an old pickup truck came rolling up and three men got out.

I yelled, "Help! Help!"

I saw them look over toward the golf cart. I know they were surprised to see a golf cart, and even more surprised to see one with people in it. One of the guys came over. I told him we had been stuck there all night. It turned out this was the cleaning crew who had come to pick up the place.

The man said, "I don't know that much about fixing golf carts."

"That's okay," I said, "If you will just call my brother Jim Bell, he can come out here and fix us up so we can get home."

About an hour later Jim drove up.

"What are you guys doing still here at the drive in?"

I told him, "We didn't mean to still be here. We sure are glad to see you!"

It turned out to be a loose wire on one of the batteries that caused the golf cart not to start. One little loose wire and we were stranded.

20 ⚐ Yellow Bucket

IT HAPPENED THE SUMMER BEFORE I started first grade. Dad came home from the doctor's office with a scary prognosis and a list of inconvenient instructions. He had injured his ankle and developed an ulcer that took up his ankle bone and a big part of the side of his foot. Our whole family saw Dr. Feild as our primary care physician. Dr. Feild's office was only a few blocks from our house, and Mom and Dad could drive there in their wheelchairs.

Our dining table was one of those old-style aluminum ones with matching vinyl cushioned chairs. I overheard Mom and Dad talking about his doctor visit from that kitchen table.

Dad said, "Dr. Feild said the foot has to come off." I told him "No way you're taking off my foot! He said he would give me two weeks. We have to do all of this at least until then."

Dad's long residence in the family recliner started right away. His foot had to be elevated all the time. Also came the endless parade of buckets of hot water for his foot to soak in. Mom ran the bathtub water as hot as she could get it. Then she filled the yellow bucket and dumped in some Epsom salts and some hydrogen peroxide. Dad had to soak his foot in that concoction forever. I was appointed to carry the bucket from the bathroom into the living room and help Dad lower the recliner and put his foot in. I can still remember the smell of the Epsom salts and the medicine Mom used to treat Dad's foot.

The good part of this for six-year-old me was, while his foot soaked, I got to sit in the chair next to Dad. The recliner had plenty of room for both of us. Afterward, Mom dried his foot and put some medicine on it, then she replaced the gauze bandage and taped it down.

The sight of Dad's ankle was awful. I had never seen anything like that in my short six years. I wondered how it got that bad so fast. One night, sitting in the recliner next to Dad, I got brave enough to ask him what would happen if he lost his foot. I wasn't sure exactly what that meant.

He said, "I'll have to go to the hospital. The doctor will cut off my foot and bandage up my leg."

I sat there trying to imagine Dad without his foot.

I asked, "Then how can you stand up?"

He said, "I'll have to just stand on the other foot."

I couldn't imagine that. "What do they do with feet that they cut off?"

"They bury them in the feet graveyard," he said.

This was all too much for me, so I didn't ask any more questions. Dad soaked his foot four times a day. He stayed in the recliner with it propped up 24 hours a day. Gradually, it started looking better and he went back to the doctor. I couldn't go with him, but I watched the street and waited for him to come home. I was excited when I saw him coming because he still had both feet. Dr. Feild thought his foot looked much better. Luckily the foot amputation was on hold, and the buckets of water were ordered for another two weeks. Then another two weeks. Eventually, his ankle healed. Even today, I remember the tenacity of Dad sticking to that schedule of elevating and soaking his foot. After that, I spent the rest of my childhood wondering where the feet graveyard was.

John Bell Jr. with Dr. T.A. Feild 1985

"They bury the feet in the feet graveyard."

21 🔔 Adventure on the Rails

JOHN BELL JR. HAD A love of trains. When John was a child, he and his family lived near the railroad tracks. When he and his sisters were outside playing and the train came rumbling by, the girls were afraid of the loud sound and ran into the house. John said that since he was not able to run inside, he decided he may as well get used to the rumble and enjoy the trains.

Growing up as the child of John Bell Jr., I remember his HO scale model train layout as an ever-present fixture in our home. John's model railroad came to life through the carpentry skills of some of his friends in the model railroad club. He painted backdrop scenery on large pieces of Masonite, which was mounted to the wall behind the model railroad. I remember him painting the large pieces by turning them around and around to reach the whole piece with his paintbrush. Some of the scenes were painted from an upside-down position with a long paintbrush taped to a dowel rod. John was a master scenery creator. In exchange for help with the carpentry work on his own model layout, he helped his fellow model railroaders with the scenery on their model railroad layouts. Over the course of his career, John won awards for his model railroad scenery. He also designed model railroad kits which were produced and sold nationwide.

In his love of all things on rails, John enjoyed being involved with the Fort Smith Trolley Museum as well. He enjoyed a longtime friendship and collaboration with the Museum President, Bradley Martin. He designed a logo for the Museum and painted a mural on the wall near the Museum as part of the Art Downtown project. His final model railroad layout was donated and now lives at the Fort Smith Trolley Museum.

There was no greater joy than being the child of John Bell Jr. and having the chance to help with railroad model mountain scenery construction. Since I was small, my hands fit in spots where wadded paper formed the base for Paper Mache and plaster mountains. Dad used small molds to make rock walls and other scenery from plaster. Using a Dremel tool or an Exacto carving knife taped to a dowel rod, he further refined the piece. John often carved intricate work from five feet away using this method. His early model train layout, built on an eight-foot piece of plywood, sat in the corner of our living room. When our family moved to a house adjacent to the school grounds at Northside High School in 1979, his model railroad was reconstructed into an L-shape, using many of the same scenery and components. I remember the rules of the model railroad room were that you never touched anything for any reason. Also, whoever swept must examine the dustpan and salvage any small people or other critical railroad materials that might have ended up on the floor.

The John Bell Jr. railroad model memory that tops the list is John's epic journey to ride the Scenic Durango & Silverton train in Durango, Colorado. John and five of his railroad model club buddies loaded into a full-sized van and rolled out at the crack of dawn. Mickey Calicott was a family friend and model railroad club member who made the trip with John. He filled me in on his view of that trip.

Mickey said, "John sat in his wheelchair the whole trip, squeezing his wheelchair between the back seat and the back doors. He sat there amongst the luggage, but he had a smile on his face the whole time. He was a fun person to be around and had a great time on the trip."

Mickey said the group made three stops on the way there and camped out to save money. He said John slept in the van, while everyone else slept out under the stars.

He said, "Up there you could see a billion stars at night. It felt like you were closer to them."

When they finally boarded the train, John was the first person in a wheelchair to use the new wheelchair lift installed on the back of the train. A picture of John on the wheelchair lift was later featured on a brochure marketing the train ride. Over the years, John talked fondly of this trip and the fun they had.

I remember Dad talking about the trip. He said, "The train went around sharp curves and seemed to lean and sway and rock along. More than once I looked out of the window and saw only a cliff straight down for miles. It looked like the train could go over the side at any moment. The train went through tunnels where there seemed to be only inches of clearance and you first thought the train would have to hit the side of the tunnel."

Dad returned home with a long salt-and-pepper beard so that he was hardly recognizable. He brought presents from the Durango & Silverton Railroad for me and Mom. Later in his life, he and Mom made the trip together so she could also ride the train.

John Bell Jr. with model railroad club heading to Colorado.
Top left: Larry Batson; Al Black; Mickey Calicott.
Bottom: Gabe Peters; John Bell Jr; David McDonald.

"There was no greater joy than being the child of John Bell Jr. and having the chance to help with railroad model mountain scenery construction!"

22 ♿ Dallas-Fort Worth Airport

JOHN BELL JR. HAD A fierce belief in the equal treatment of people with disabilities. Particularly in his early years, he faced discrimination and physical barriers on a daily basis, which fueled his desire to level the playing ground. The most pressing concern was the apathy he felt existed on the part of our local, state, and national leadership regarding the rights of individuals with disabilities. The desire to eliminate this apathy led him to serve as the President of United Cerebral Palsy, Arkansas Chapter. He also served on the Arkansas State Planning and Advisory Council on Developmental Disabilities. As part of his role with those organizations, he travelled frequently across the nation in the 1970s.

Travel for individuals who use wheelchairs was then and is now still difficult. Because airplanes are not equipped with seating areas that allow people to fly while seated in their wheelchairs, the wheelchair needs to be stowed in the lower compartment of the plane with the luggage. If a person travelling in a wheelchair has a connecting flight, the airline provides a small wheelchair for the person to use while in the airport. Those wheelchairs lack batteries and motors, which means the person has to rely on a friend or on the airport staff to help them get around. These conditions caused some great difficulty for John Bell Jr. during his travels. He told this story about his experiences while travelling from Fort Smith to Washington D.C.

JOHN BELL:

In December of '75, I had to fly to Washington for a meeting with the Advisory Council on Developmental Disabilities. This meeting was a conference on how to make public travel more accessible. The irony of this was that my trip to this conference was one of the worst airline trips of my life. I had to be up at the crack of dawn to get to the airport on time. One of my friends from the Fort

Smith Jaycees, Bob Watson, agreed to take me to the airport in his pickup truck. Bob put my wheelchair in the back of his truck and loaded me into the cab. We used a couple of 2x4 boards as ramps to roll the wheelchair up into the truck.

Those boards were slick when they got wet, and you had to be careful to keep the wheels straight to stay on the boards. On the way there, it started snowing. By the time we got to the airport, my chair was covered in snow. Bob raked off the snow and plopped me in the chair. By the time we got inside, my butt was wet.

The whole place was jam packed with people already. We went inside and checked my bag. Back then, I couldn't fly with batteries in my wheelchair because they were considered hazardous material. The batteries had to be removed, and I had to arrange for someone to have a set of batteries at my destination to put in the chair. The plan was for Bob to take the batteries out of my wheelchair and store them in his garage until I got back. Then he would reinstall them when I was back home.

This little, tiny airport guy came over with one of those airport wheelchairs. The guy looked at me, at Bob, and at my chair. The guy stood there and said, "Can you get over here in this chair?"

I said, "Buddy, if I could walk over to where you are, I wouldn't need a wheelchair."

I had to show the guy how to set the brakes on the wheelchair and where to put it so I could get in it. Back then I could stand, turn around and then sit down in another chair. That was all fine, but the airport wheelchair was little so it could fit down the small isle of the airplane. If I sat in it very long, my rear end went to sleep.

This flight was from Fort Smith to DFW Airport in Dallas. It was a short flight and a little plane. Back then the small planes parked on the tarmac, and I had to get someone to haul me up the steps into the plane. Bob wheeled me outside onto the tarmac in the spitting snow. I didn't want to be all bundled up on the flight, so I wasn't wearing a very big coat. I was freezing. The wind was blowing snow so hard the flakes stung my face. Bob picked me up, hauled me up the steps into the plane, and plopped me down in a seat. For better or worse, there I was.

This flight was so full I didn't know how the plane could haul all of us off the ground. I knew we were in trouble when I saw the stewardess sit down and buckle up. The wind batted the plane around so much it felt like a roller coaster ride. Finally, the pilot said we were landing at DFW airport. I could see the runway coming up to the plane at an angle. It looked like we would hit it sideways. At the last minute, the pilot flew parallel to the ground and then, "Slam!" The plane hit the runway. It careened around in the wind. Then I heard some squealing tires and the plane jerked to a stop. People were looking white-faced.

The pilot just said, "Welcome to DFW airport."

They always let everyone else off the plane first, and then the crippled people last. I sat there forever and then came this huge airport guy with a buns-pinching wheelchair. He didn't even make any conversation. He just picked me up and plopped me in the chair. It wasn't snowing in Dallas, but the wind was sharp, and it felt like it could snow any minute. I was glad to get inside the airport. The big guy wheeled me just inside and sat me there against a post.

I said, "I'm going to need someone to take me to my connecting gate."

So, he says, "Yes, Mr. Bell, someone will be coming to get you."

Famous last words. I had about a two-hour layover. In an airport that big, two hours was just enough time to be able to get to the gate for the next flight. I sat there for about 30 minutes. I was too far from the customer service desk to even ask about an attendant. I looked around and saw this guy sitting there with a drink in one hand and a white cane in the other hand. I started talking with him. His name was Jack. I figured out he was on the same flight I needed to be on.

He said, "I got drafted for this disability meeting in D.C. Anyway, I figure its free food if nothing else."

I told him, "Well I'm supposed to speak at that meeting for United Cerebral Palsy. If I can get there…"

We both needed help finding the gate because he couldn't see to read the gate numbers, and I was in a wheelchair with no batteries. We decided the airline people weren't coming to take us to the next gate. I looked at my ticket and figured out which gate we needed, and it was all the way across the place.

"Well heck," he said. "We better get going if we're gonna make that flight!"

"We gotta flag someone down," I said.

"Forget that. You can see, you just tell me where we're going." He gave me his cane and said, "Here, hold this." He took hold of the back of my wheelchair and started pushing me through the airport. "You'll have to tell me where we're going…"

He did not waste any time. He was pushing me, people were dodging us, and he was hollering, "VIP person here! Late for a flight! Make way!" He was almost running.

I was yelling, "To the right!"

He veered a little to the right, but not far enough and people dodged.

I started saying, "Right! Right! Right! Left! Left! Left!"

He steered at my command. I was watching the gate numbers and yelling, "108!" He pushed faster. "112!"

We finally got to the gate. That was just the beginning.

When you're a crippled man on a cross country trip, and have no batteries for your wheelchair, you have to be careful what you drink because you can't get in any of the bathrooms. So, when we finally landed in Washington DC, it was past 9:00 pm and I was ready for the bathroom big time. I waited for everyone else to deplane, and then sat in the airport in one of the tiny airport wheelchairs waiting for my chair to come off the plane. A guy who was titled 'chairman of access and accommodations' for the Council on Developmental Disabilities conference I was attending was supposed to arrange for some batteries to be at the airport for my wheelchair so I could get around. Lo and behold, my wheelchair was unloaded, and I finally was able to get in it, but Mr. Chairman showed up with no batteries.

He came walking up saying, "Hello, Mr. Bell. Welcome to Washington D.C. I have a van waiting to take you to the hotel."

I said, "Okay, but what about my batteries for my wheelchair?"

He said, "We've arranged for ABC Company to bring some batteries to the hotel in the morning for you."

I was livid. "Those batteries were supposed to be here at the airport when I got off the plane. I've been travelling since 7:00 this morning. I have had nothing to eat or drink all day, and I need to go to the bathroom! I can't get around on my own without those batteries. Now how are we going to solve this problem?"

"Well Mr. Bell," he said, "…let me make some phone calls…"

He disappeared.

When he came back, he said, "There aren't any battery companies open right now. The best we can do is to have some delivered tomorrow, but they will be at the hotel by 7:00 am."

I said, "That's totally unacceptable. You people knew I needed those batteries when I got off the plane. I can't get to the van, I can't get to the bathroom, I can't get around in my room at the hotel, I can't do anything without those batteries."

"Well sir, I can push you in the wheelchair."

"You sure can," I said. "I'll need you to stay with me until I can get those batteries installed. That means, you have to push me EVERYWHERE. Including the bathroom. Do you understand?"

"Yes Sir Mr. Bell."

"Call your wife and tell her you won't be home tonight."

He got me in the van, and we drove to the hotel. He pushed me into my room, and into the bathroom. I had him set the brake on the chair, and I was able to take care of my bathroom business. Then he wheeled me out and back to the room.

The man looked tired and sheepish.

I didn't care.

Then he asked, "Do you need something to eat Mr. Bell? I don't think the restaurant is open, but I'll go get something for you."

"No, just get me over by the bed and I'm just going to get some sleep." I said, "I hope your room is nearby in case I need to go to the bathroom in the night!"

I gave him a room key so he could get in early to help me get up. Later I found out he had slept on the floor in the hallway with his back up against the wall.

I finally got some batteries put in my chair and I was able to get around by myself. When I got to speak at the meeting, I talked about access to air travel and the need for air carriers to create spaces on the planes where people in wheelchairs could travel in their own wheelchairs instead of having to get into an airline seat. I talked about the oversight with the batteries at this conference as an example of an issue that would be resolved by creating such access.

When it was time to fly home, I was met with a problem of a different kind. There was a snowstorm, and the airline couldn't fly me to Dallas. There was no straight flight to Fort Smith from Washington D.C.

At the ticket counter I told them, "I can't go anywhere like someone who doesn't use a wheelchair. I have to have my wheelchair and batteries, and I have to be at a hotel with a bathroom big enough that I can get in and out of it. How can we solve this problem?"

The airline ticket person asked, "Do you have any family anywhere else in the country who can put you up for the night? We will fly you anywhere we can land and then get you home to Fort Smith tomorrow."

I started thinking. Then I remembered my friend Frankie Dennie. I met her through United Cerebral Palsy. Frankie's daughter had Cerebral Palsy. She and her husband had created a center for handicapped children. She had a daughter and a son and lived in Tulsa.

I called Frankie. "Frankie?" I said, "Do you remember how you said to call you if I ever needed anything?"

"John Bell!" She said, "What's going on? Where are you?"

"I don't know if you can help me, but here's my predicament." I explained everything to her.

Frankie said her son could pick me up in his truck at the airport. I was saved! Saved from sleeping all night in the airport! Saved from spending countless hours in a narrow airport wheelchair! The airline flew me to Tulsa. The plane touched down in heavy snow. I didn't have any batteries in my wheelchair, so Frankie's son pushed me everywhere. He took me to their house, and I slept in Frankie's daughter's room. They took good care of me. They took good care of me even though Frankie's husband was very ill, and she was taking care of him. That night Frankie and her son had me, her daughter, and her husband to take care of. I owe her and her family for that to this day. I was never so glad to finally get home from a trip in my life.

Jim Bell on Washington D.C. trip 1975

I said, "Ok, but what about the batteries for my wheelchair?"

23 🔔 Washington D.C.

THIS IS THE STORY DAD told about his next trip to Washington D.C. He was determined to avoid the issues he experienced during the last trip.

JOHN BELL:

The last trip I made to Washington DC was such a harrowing experience, I decided to avoid flying on my own if possible. When I needed to go to Washington again, I drafted my brother, Jim, to take me. I told him I would be in meetings all day, but in the evening, we could go see the sights. Jim had a pickup truck with a camper shell. We loaded my wheelchair in the back and headed out. It's a long way to Washington D.C. from Fort Smith in a pickup truck. We decided we could spend the night in campgrounds on the way to save some money. At night, we unloaded my wheelchair and slept in the back of the truck.

One night we were sleeping, when we heard, "Tap, tap, tappity tap tap taptaptaptap!" on the top of the camper shell. It was a nice sound to hear when you're trying to sleep.

I woke up and said, "What's that?"

Jim said, "It's just rain."

"Oh, okay."

We both realized it at the same time. My wheelchair was outside getting wet. Wet wheelchairs can short out!

Jim was out of that truck like a shot. "Junior, you gotta get up."

He got me up and put me in the cab of the truck.

Then, in the rain and in the middle of the night, Jim loaded my wheelchair in the back of the truck to keep it dry.

We spent the rest of the night with both of us trying to sleep in the cab. The next morning our first stop was to buy a tarp to put over the wheelchair.

When we got to D.C., the conference was at the Washington Hilton Hotel. The hotel lobby was fancy and plush and so were the rooms. The doorway to the bathrooms was still too narrow for my wheelchair to get through. Back then, hotels seldom had any rooms that were accessible for people with wheelchairs. So, Jim brought tools to remove the bathroom door so that my wheelchair fit through.

LISA BELL WILSON:

I talked to my Uncle Jim about this story that Dad had told for years. I asked him about this trip to Washington D.C. Jim remembered taking him on that trip very well.

"I was there in that fancy place with my hammer banging on those door hinges," Jim said. "I waited for someone to come and tell us we couldn't take off the door. I said to him, 'Junior, what if someone comes in and says we can't be taking off this door?'"

"Just let them come in and try to tell us that," John told me.

"When we got ready to check out, I put the door back on."

While John was in meetings, I hung out in the room. In the evening, we went all through Washington D.C. One of John's favorite places that we visited was the Smithsonian Air and Space Museum. All those museums were accessible, even back then. We also went to Williamsburg and Jamestown. I think John enjoyed the history of those towns even more than he did the Washington D.C. area."

John Bell Jr. at the United States Capitol in Washington D.C. 1975

"Back then, hotels seldom had any rooms that were accessible for people with wheelchairs. Jim brought tools to take the door off of the bathroom so I could get in."

24 ⚜ Near Drowning of the Crippled

LAKE TENKILLER WAS THE BIGGEST and most beautiful place I had ever seen in all of my eight years. At that time, our family had had few vacations, and the prospect of a great campout on the lake was the most exciting event of my life. Dad's friend Bob Watson, Dad's business partner Butch Priest, and my Uncle Jim and his family, all went on this campout with us. We loaded up tents, lawn chairs and way too much food and headed out. I remember that a pickup truck loaded with my parents' two wheelchairs and various other items made us look a lot like the Beverly Hillbillies. I didn't care.

Unable to wait to get in the water, I ran and put on my swimsuit as soon as I got out of the truck. The guys were erecting the biggest cabin tent I had ever seen. Running on the hot blacktop-paved pathway, my feet were literally burning off. Finally, I came to the sandy beach spot where the swim area was marked with orange floating buoys. That water was cool and felt amazing. The bottom of the lake felt cold and squishy under my feet. Wondering what might be living in that mud, I pulled my feet up from the bottom and floated there with my swim ring, looking up at a couple of white fluffy clouds and blue sky. After approximately forever, I decided it was time to head back to camp and find something to eat.

The whole place looked like a city of tents. Swim toys were piled up and ice chest coolers were everywhere. Mom was talking to Uncle Jim's wife, and Dad was sitting at the picnic table, shirt off, eating a hot dog. I had never seen Dad sit outside with no shirt, so I was wondering if that was a thing you could do. He saw me coming over with a plate, and asked, "How was the water?"

I said, "It's beautiful. The water is cool."

"Good," he said. "I'm about to go swimming."

I almost choked on my hotdog. "What?" I asked, "Can you swim?"

"No, but I probably won't drown." He did not look like someone who should try to swim at all. He looked like someone who should stay on dry ground in his wheelchair.

"Dad, it's pretty deep out there, I don't think you should try to get in."

"I'll have a life raft," he told me, "…it'll be fine."

No more had I finished my Ruffles when Uncle Jim, Butch Priest and Bob Watson headed out to the swim area with Dad. They gave me two life rafts and a swim ring to carry, and I trotted along behind them. I know we all looked ridiculous.

We got to the edge of the water, and those guys grabbed Dad under the shoulders and hauled him out of his wheelchair into the water. I couldn't believe it. They hauled him out to where he could sit on the bottom, in some fashion, and I brought the swimming rings. Dad was pushed and pulled, water splashed up and over his head, and finally he was situated on a raft with his arms over the middle of the thing. The raft bent in the middle and looked like the letter V with Dad in the middle. Then, the guys proceeded to haul him out to deeper water. I had never seen Dad in the water like that, and I was afraid for him. I didn't know how much of a risk taker he had always been. Everyone was laughing but me.

Then it happened. Jim was on one side of him and Bob on the other. Dad moved somehow, and just flipped over and disappeared under the water! Those two lunged and grabbed him. They hauled him back to the surface. I was sent to get more swim toys. Finally, Dad was situated with a swim ring around each arm and his middle across the swim raft, looking like a V with two Os.

He was saying, "I'm good. It's cool."

I couldn't believe it. Dad stayed in the water forever. Finally, those guys decided they wanted to go eat, but Dad still didn't want to go in. I stayed out there with him in the swimming area until the sun started going down and Uncle Jim came to see if Dad wanted to get out.

Dad said, "No, I'm good."

We stayed. He floated. I swam around him. Fish nibbled his legs. Fish jumped in the water. People all got out of the swimming area and went to their camps. Finally, Jim and Bob waded out into the lake, and hauled Dad out of the water and sat him in his wheelchair. I was relieved to see him back safely on the ground. That trip was the only time I saw Dad swim in the lake, and the most fun I believe the two of us ever had together.

John Bell Jr. and Jim Bell at Lake Tenkiller State Park 1973

"I was sent to get more swim toys."

25 ♫ Family Reunion

FAMILY IS OFTEN DEFINED AS the people you love who stay nearby and have an interest in your wellbeing. A real family is not always only people who are related to a person by lineage. John and Maxine Bell were people who became family to many. Cornell Barker came to be family through his work as a Certified Nurse Assistant with the Area Agency on Aging. Although he was not related by ancestry, the bond between Cornell and our family was stronger than the bond in some families with blood relation.

As he aged, John Bell Jr. became unable to transfer from his wheelchair to his bed without falling. Since he was such a proud and independent person, it took a lot for John to ask the Agency on Aging for help with a personal care aid. One of the first people to enter our home in that capacity was Cornell.

Cornell made John feel comfortable in asking for the assistance he needed. In turn, Dad became something like a second father to Cornell, who worked for our family for several years. Later, Cornell left the Area Agency for another job, but he continued to come help Dad on his own time. When other aides came, Cornell drove by the house at night to make sure Dad was in bed. If the living room light was still on, Cornell would stop and check on Dad. When our family needed to go out of town, Cornell sometimes travelled with us to make sure John's needs were met. We made many family trips and have memories that would have been impossible without Cornell.

Maxine was one of nine children born to Lucille Skinner Tincher and Arthur Tincher. Those nine children had twenty-one children. It was quite a clan, spread out all over the nation. Every summer saw our Skinner Family clan gathered at Lake Tenkiller State Park in Oklahoma. Some years we were sixty people, taking over the park, all in blue matching shirts. John and Maxine Bell rented a handicapped accessible cabin at nearby Greenleaf Lake. That allowed them to be able to spend the night and avoid driving the fifty miles back and forth to Fort Smith during the reunion activities. Cornell was invited to come along as well because John needed his help. He was also invited because he was family. He was our blue shirt family.

Cornell had his own family in nearby Muskogee. He would visit them and then come back to Tenkiller in time to help Dad. Late nights on the lake found Cornell studying scriptures on the front porch of the cabin.

The Reunion schedule included Sunday night as kids' night, with a pinata and other treats for the children. Burgers were grilled and games played. Everyone showed up and donned blue shirts, taking over the playground and swimming pool. Cornell joined all of us for fun and burgers. Maybe too much fun…

You know, you don't always get to choose your family, but you love them anyway. Cousin Ginger was one of our more colorful family members. Everywhere she went, Ginger carried a big, insulated mug full of some questionable substance. During the kids' night activities on this trip, Cornell was there with all of the family, perched on railing around the pavilion. Soon Ginger was seen sitting next to him, watching children swing a bat at a particularly stubborn pinata. Ginger scooted closer and closer to Cornell.

Finally, the pinata was bruised but not even cracked a little, so some of the men decided to help break it, and Cornell was much obliged to lend his hand. With candy and burgers eaten, all returned to the cabins to get some rest before the main family reunion activities the next day.

Cornell and Dad were overheard talking on the front porch over glasses of tea. Cornell said, "You'll never believe what happened tonight."

Dad said, "What was it?"

Cornell said, "Ginger came over and sat right next to me. I scooted down, but she moved too and got closer. Then she started talking to me. She propositioned me! I couldn't believe it. I really didn't know what to do."

Dad said, "What? What did you say to her?"

Cornell said, "I told her I wouldn't want to make her boyfriend mad. She just said, 'I don't have a boyfriend!' I had to get up and get out of there."

Dad said, "Well you never know with her what's going to happen. Just watch your back!"

Later that night, we all went for a walk through the campground. We looked at the lake and all of the stars. On the way back to the cabin, Dad was telling Cornell, "I think I see Ginger hiding in the bushes. You better book it out of here."

Those two laughed like they were in high school.

The next day, the family all met at the community building at Lake Tenkiller. The family ate all day long, because that's what we do. People were in the pool, on the playground, everywhere. Part of the reunion activities was always an auction where items everyone brought were auctioned off. The auction helped pay for the reunion for the next year. Everyone knew that Cornell had come with us on his own time to help Dad. Dad paid him for the extra time. So, the family took up a special collection to help with that expense. That evening, again on the front porch, Dad and Cornell were talking.

"Here's some extra money for your trouble coming all the way here," Dad said to him.

"I came because I wanted to," Cornell said. "You don't have to pay me anything extra."

Dad said, "Oh yes, I do. Besides, this money came from the family. They appreciate you coming." Then he said, "You know where most of this money came from don't you?"

Cornell said, "No."

Dad teased, "Out of Ginger's purse!"

This event was one for the family reunion history books. This single event set apart this reunion from all of the others and made a special family memory.

John Bell Jr. with Cornell Barker 2012

26 ♫ Art Downtown Kids

IN THE LATE 1980s, JOHN Bell Jr. worked for the Western Arkansas Employment Development Agency in a project called Art Downtown. It was a program to provide jobs for low-income high school students, funded by the Comprehensive Employment and Training Act. John supervised the students and trained them to paint artwork on downtown buildings to beautify the area and attract tourism. It was during his work in this capacity that I got to really see what a talented and diverse artist he was.

The Art Downtown Project was housed in an old building on Garrison Avenue with a crumbling entryway and huge plate glass windows. The spot used to be a furniture store, and some old furniture was still in the very back of the open room John worked in. As his daughter, I was occasionally asked to take lunch to him. My orientation to the Art Downtown project was a memorable experience.

I opened the heavy door to this cavernous workspace. Immediately a mixture of the smells of paint and musty old buildings rushed out. The ceiling seemed to be held up by a series of columns arranged around the room. The floor was covered in 1960s' linoleum squares in an alternating antique white and a salmon color. Dotted around the room were metal folding chairs and a couple of large fans.

The space was a bustle of activity. Eleven young people were busy at work. A wall approximately 10 feet long boasted a mockup drawing of one of Dad's paintings. The drawing was covered with a grid pattern of three-foot squares. In front of the drawing were step stools and sawhorses.

On another wall was a painting with clouds and other shapes that were not discernable as anything in particular. Kids were working on both walls. A long wooden folding table in the middle of the room was covered with paint cans, tarps and other art supplies.

When I walked in, Dad was supervising two kids who were painting on the small wall. He was situated between the two groups of kids so he could see everything going on.

They were painting with large sponges soaked in white paint.

Dad was telling them things like, "No, you need more paint on that sponge. Okay, now lightly touch the wall with the sponge, and gently swipe up."

I stood there watching all the activity.

I said, "You guys have a lot going on here."

Dad said, "Well, this is our practice wall here, where they're learning how to paint."

I asked, "Why is that grid pattern drawn all over your painting?"

He explained, "The grid breaks the painting up into small paintings that are all about three feet square. They study each square and learn to paint what is in each square on the practice wall. Then they will paint the whole thing in here for practice. We do the same process outside on the real thing."

It really was amazing.

Dad addressed the kids on the practice wall, "Let's show her what you've learned."

I watched as the kids' covered sponges in white and gray paint. They tapped the sponges onto the wall alternately to make clouds.

Finally, one kid said, "See? John Bell Clouds!" and the other said, "By remote!"

They were right. He supervised those kids, addressed some behavior problems, and managed a work area in a downtown area where homeless people sometimes stole their supplies. He worked in the heat and in the cold. From a wheelchair, and without the use of his hands, he coached those kids to paint beautiful murals on the walls of the downtown buildings. When each one was done, the kids signed their names.

In the Spring of 1996, a tornado destroyed some of the buildings that held the paintings, including a portion of the wall at the Fort Smith Trolley Museum. Dad and the kids found the painted bricks from the painting on the Fort Smith Trolley Museum wall. He showed them how to reassemble the wall. And then they fixed the broken places to restore the painting. Those kids learned to paint, some carpentry and a little masonry skill. They learned to work together and to respect authority.

Gaining a picture of the job Dad did while working on that project made me think about his bid to work as a classroom teacher. I was reminded that the school superintendent and others thought he would not be able to handle a classroom full of kids. Part of his job in this work was to make sure the kids behaved as they would need to on a job. He said he had a few kids who tested his authority and a few who just didn't want to do the job.

What he said overall about the discipline issues with those kids was, "If a kid stepped too far out of line, the others really took care of it in most cases. Many of these kids didn't have a father figure at home. They had respect for me and didn't want others to be disrespectful. They were all good kids."

After that project was discontinued, several of Dad's 'Art Downtown Kids' kept in contact with him through the years. In his later years, Dad called on a few of them to help with jobs around the house. He really loved those kids, and they loved him and respected him like a father.

> *"He supervised those kids, managed some behavior problems, and managed a work area in a downtown where homeless people sometimes stole their supplies."*

27 🔔 Lefty

A CERTAIN RADIANCE EMANATED FROM John Bell Jr. when talking about his experience working with the Art Downtown project. He was proud of the kids he worked with on that project and said many times that he enjoyed seeing the participants gain confidence in themselves. John had a fierce protective spirit for those in his care, and the vulnerability of the work area with his 'Art Downtown kids' was not lost on him. When discussing his work in that project, he once said, "I had to gauge the maturity level of each kid and their ability to take responsibility, and to give them only as much as they could handle. The truth was, I needed them to get the work done, and they needed me." One student who participated in the program was Jason Gilkey.

Regarding Jason, John said, "Jason was very mature for his age. He took on lots of responsibility and was helpful with the other kids too."

When working on art projects with adolescents in an area open to the public, many things can happen. One of Dad's stories about his Art Downtown adventures concerned Lefty the homeless man.

John said, "One day we were beginning a mural on a wall and working with white paint. We went to lunch and came back to find our paint was gone. We didn't have that much budget to work with, so I was furious. I was thinking, 'Who would steal a bunch of white paint from us?' I went looking for the paint thief and took Jason with me. It didn't take long to see, painted in huge white letters, 'Lefty Was Here!' So, we went looking for Lefty."

I talked to Jason about this experience working for the Art Downtown project. Jason said, "Mr. Bell and I walked along until we saw a homeless man wondering around under the bridge. He was drunk and partly covered in white paint. Mr. Bell didn't want me to approach the man, but I wasn't afraid of that type of stuff. I walked along parallel to him. He saw me and finally wandered off, and I got the paint. There wasn't enough paint left for us to finish our project. Mr. Bell sent me to Sherwin Williams on my scooter to get more paint. I was the only one who had transportation. That was a big responsibility for a 14-year-old!"

I asked Jason about Lefty. He said, "We used a grocery cart to take our paint from the Art Downtown building to the mural. We had gone to lunch and left the cart and the paint at the mural. We never left the paint unattended again."

28 🔔 Old Blue

OLD BLUE WAS A USED 1980 Chevy Mark III van that Dad purchased. This was the first vehicle my parents owned since the golf cart they used when I was a baby. Blue already had a bunch of miles on her, but dad scraped together the money to buy it and get it outfitted to be driven from a wheelchair. It was about 1985 and I had just started college. Those two had been stuck at home for years. Blue, to them, was freedom of the open road. They were able to get away and do things that other people take for granted. After procuring Old Blue, they were never home on weekends.

    I found this out the hard way when I headed home for the weekend looking for some home cooking. I packed myself up, broke, hungry, and homesick and drove to Fort Smith to find the house empty. Back then there were no cell phones, so I just hung out thinking they had gone to a movie. I did laundry. I ate all the food in the house. The sun went down and came back up on Sunday. I feared the worst. Finally, with my car loaded for the trip back to school, I heard the crunch of tires on gravel in the driveway.

    I felt foolish but I couldn't help but rush outside.

    Mom was happily unloading items from the van.

    "Where have you two been? I've been here all weekend. I was worried!"

    Dad said, "We went camping."

    I couldn't even imagine that. I said, "Camping?"

    "Yes," he said. "Lots of people go camping. Next time you want to come home you better call first."

John Bell Jr. and "Old Blue" 1985

"Those two had been stuck at home for years and Blue, to them, was the freedom of the open road."

29 🔔 Christmas with the Yankee Dog Mayor

FAMILY TIES ARE THE GLUE that holds us together, in good times and bad. A common thread running throughout the tapestry that was his life was John's relationship with his sister Lillian and her family. As it is with family, the two relied on each other in various capacities throughout the years. As children, they relied on each other sometimes for mere survival.

He became a well-known local artist. She married Bill Kropp II, and became a very well-respected teacher, touching the lives of countless young people. Even as adults, the two had good times and bad times together, but their love for each other was ever present. John cherished the time spent with Lillian and her family during the holidays most. Of the many Christmas memories built on that bedrock, this is one of the most cherished.

The economic downturn of the early 1980s hit home in a most personal way for the Kropp household. Bill Kropp II had worked for Garrison Furniture for years. The company folded and he lost his job. With two kids in college, he was on the unemployment line. The John Bell Jr. household was all too familiar with the circumstance of being unemployed, and John wanted to lend support where he could. As was the case almost every year, our family was invited to join the Kropp family for a holiday meal.

John said to Maxine, "Well they invited us over, and we need to go and see if we can cheer them up some."

Sitting around the table in the Kropps' smallest dining area, we drank coffee. On the discussion table was the unemployment situation as well as the Kropps' traditional birthday celebration with the Vines family. Regarding this celebration, Bill said, "We always try to top what we did last year at the Vines' house. Last year was huge, and I was already not sure how to top it. Now, with all this job hunting going on, I haven't felt like thinking about what to do."

The situation seemed bleak, but Bill had already laid some groundwork for this year's events. I drank coffee and listened as a new plan began to unfold.

The backstory is that Bill Kropp II was good friends with the Mayor of Fort Smith, Bill Vines. The Vines lived across the street from the Kropps, and the two played tennis together at the Hardscrabble Country Club. Bill Vines bemoaned having a Christmas Eve birthday, saying that he never got birthday presents, he only got Christmas presents. As a remedy, Bill and Lillian Kropp gave Vines birthday presents every year on Christmas eve. The gift was always a can of tennis balls. Every year, they hatched a plan to disguise the fact that his birthday gift was once again tennis balls. The birthday tradition became more and more elaborate each year.

The previous year the Kropps hosted a Japanese exchange student named Kyo. Since Bill Vines was originally from "Up North," the Kropps called him the Yankee Dog Mayor. So last year, the Kropps set up a mock trial where Vines was found guilty of being a Yankee Dog. He was sentenced to death by the dumiwidget. This apparatus was a leaf blower loaded with tennis balls.

To carry out his sentence, both families took Vines outside, blindfolded him, and turned on the blower. Vines was pelted with tennis balls. Someone took a picture and caught on camera a tennis ball in midair about to hit Vines.

Following the great trial, Bill Kropp took the photo to the photo shop and had it blown up. The enlarged photo showed a sharp image in the very middle of the picture, with a tennis ball and Vines. The image was blurry on the edges. Bill had the photo made into a puzzle. When Kyo finished school and went back to Japan, Bill sent those middle puzzle pieces with her. Kyo put the pieces in a small box and wrote on the outside, "To Yankee Dog Mayor Bill Vines" and mailed them back to Fort Smith.

Throughout the year, Bill gave puzzle pieces to salesmen who met with him at Garrison Furniture. In turn, they mailed the pieces back to Fort Smith from all over the nation, addressed to Bill Vines. All year, Vines was getting puzzle pieces from all over the nation, but he didn't know who was sending them or why. The image on the pieces was too blurry to make out. Bill Kropp didn't know that Vines was even getting the pieces until he saw an article in Tom Blake's column in the Southwest Times Record. The article stated that the mayor was receiving puzzle pieces from all over the nation and that it was a mystery…

Fast Forward, a plan built on this groundwork was hatching. The new plan landed on the front porch of a vacant, run-down old house that sat next door to Dad's art studio on North B Street. Dad's landlord also owned the old house. Dad contacted the landlord and got permission to use the old house that night. He found that the house was being renovated and the power was on.

Next, Bill and Dad started thinking about how to use the old house. The issue at hand was how to get Bill Vines to the old house and how to involve tennis balls. What evolved was the idea of a story that an old lady was holed up in her old house in the cold and would not come out. Bill Kropp thought that Vines would come to the rescue of an old lady in that situation.

It just so happened that dad's brother, Jim Bell, was a firefighter for the City of Fort Smith. If they could use a fire truck to transport Vines to the old house, he just might buy the whole story. Dad went to work contacting the Fort Smith Fire Chief Pettway to discuss this proposal. Dad explained the whole plan to Pettway and asked if they could have Jim come in a fire truck to transport Vines.

Pettway said, "I wouldn't mind Jim being involved in this, but the City has a strict policy that no civilians can ride in Fire Department vehicles."

I wondered how Dad would get around that one.

He said, "Well, the only person riding in the vehicle with Jim would be the mayor. He's not exactly considered a civilian."

Pettway said, "You have a point. Well, he wouldn't be able to bring a fire engine, because we never know when we will need those, but he could come in a regular fire truck."

"That's all we'll need," Dad said, and it was done.

With the hard part arranged, the rest of the plan fell in place. It unfolded as follows. Just like every other year, the Kropps went to the Vines' house for Christmas Eve dinner. Mother, Dad and I waited at the Kropps' house. Dad was near the phone.

When they arrived at the Vines' house, the Kropps and the Vines families sat talking about Christmas. Bill told Vines that he had been so focused on job hunting he had not done anything about the Birthday situation and had barely arranged Christmas for his family.

They all ate and talked about this predicament, and then the phone rang. On the other end of the phone was Dad, posing as Fire Chief Pettway.

Dad said, "Good evening, and Merry Christmas. This is Chief Pettway. We have a situation I need to talk to Bill about."

Mrs. Vines then came in to tell Bill Vines that the fire chief was on the phone. Mayor Vines excused himself.

Dad said, "Good evening, Bill. This is Pettway. I really hate to bother you at home on Christmas Eve, but we have a situation we're dealing with, and I need your help."

Vines said, "Of course, what's the situation?"

Dad said, "Well, there is an elderly lady who probably in the beginning stages of Alzheimer's who is in danger."

Vines asked, "What sort of danger?"

Dad said, "Her family has arranged for her to go to a residential care facility, and she's holed up in her old house with no heat on, and she won't come out. We're trying to get her to go to a relative's house until a spot is ready for her at the facility."

Vines said, "It should be easy to contact Entergy and get them to turn on the power to her home in an emergency situation."

Dad said, "Yes, we're already working on getting power restored. Our major concern is for her safety. It's not safe for her to be in that old house alone. The lady says she is a longtime fan of Mayor Vines, and that she will come out if you personally come and ask her to come out. She says if the mayor is there, she will know it's safe. Like I said, she's probably in the beginning of Alzheimer's. I know it's late, and it's Christmas Eve, but we could send a car to pick you up. It shouldn't take long for you to just talk to her."

Vines said, "Okay, I'll be glad to talk to her. I'll get my coat and be ready."

Dad said, "Thank you for taking time away from your family to help this old lady. We'll send a truck over."

Grabbing his coat, Bill Vines then went into the living room where his family were all visiting with the Kropps. He told them the story about the old lady. He said he really needed to go take care of this and he was sorry about leaving their company. Of course, the Kropps encouraged him to go ahead and take care of this important situation.

While getting his coat, it occurred to Vines that someone was trying to get him alone and away from his residence. In his coat pocket he had stowed his derringer pistol, just in case. About that time, Vines looked out of the bedroom window and saw an actual Fort Smith fire truck pull up outside. Vines decided he didn't need the gun, and that this was a legitimate situation.

Jim Bell came to the door and escorted Mr. Vines to the truck. The plan was for Jim to drive first to the wrong side of town to buy time for everyone to leave the Vines' house and to get to the old house and hide in the background. As Jim pulled away from the Vines' house, the dispatcher came on the radio saying the address to go to was 1516 South B Street. Jim drove to South B Street although he really needed to be at North B Street to buy time.

In the meantime, the Kropp's swung by and picked me up at their house and everyone went over to the old house, hid our cars and went inside. The house had about five steps up to a large wooden porch. The front door had a big, glass window and opened to a long entryway. Upon entering the front door, it was only seven or eight steps to another door that opened to a large closet.

Lillian Kropp hid in that closet with the door closed, can of tennis balls in hand. The rest of us hid in a room just off the entry way. We could barely see the entry door from where we hid.

About fifteen minutes passed, and then we saw Bill Vines and Jim come up on the porch and begin knocking on the door. It didn't look like they were going to come in. Someone from our hiding place tried to get in a position where Jim could see us motion him to come in without Vines seeing. Finally, they opened the front door and came to the entryway.

As soon as the front door opened Lillian, from her hiding place in her little room, started a low and fierce moaning.

Vines went to the door and said, "Ma'am, this is Mayor Vines. We need you to come on out of there and ride with us."

More moaning. She was saying something in such a voice that you just couldn't tell what it was. It was two words over and over.

Later, Vines said that he was just then thinking about how the fireman was standing aside from the door and that he himself was standing directly in front of the door. Vines was thinking about how a shot coming through the door would hit him square on and would miss the fireman.

Right then, Lillian swung open the door, thrust out her hand with the can of tennis balls in it and yelled out a now clear "Tennis Balls!"

We watched from the shadows and Vines grabbed his chest.

He stumbled back flailing his arms a bit. He gasped out "What the…" and we all came out saying "Tennis Balls! Tennis Balls!"

After all that action, everyone got back in their cars and headed back to the Vines' house. When they all went inside, I hid in the car wearing a Japanese Kimono, holding the box of center puzzle pieces in a mailing box from Japan. Once they were all inside and comfortable, I stood on the porch in my Kimono and rang the bell. Someone answered the door.

"I have a package for the Yankee Dog Mayor," I said.
He came to the door, and I gave him the box from Japan. We all went inside and saw the realization on Vines' face about the puzzle pieces. Those middle pieces told the story of him, the deadly tennis ball from last year, and all the puzzle pieces he had been receiving all year.

Then we all went over to the Kropps' house, where Dad and Mom sat waiting. A commemorative picture was taken of everyone, and with Dad operating the phone.

30 ♙ Oh! Lovely Christmas Tree!

THE CHRISTMAS SEASON WAS ALWAYS a special time in the John Bell Jr. household. My earliest childhood memories of Christmas at home are not individual memories but something that is the embodiment of the whole holiday experience. The season seemed to burst with the color of the green Christmas tree, twinkling lights and packages wrapped in every color. I remember classical style Christmas music coming from Dad's big Sony stereo speakers. The smell of baking pies floated in the air. Even today, the smell of mincemeat pie in the oven transports me back to the John Bell Jr. household…and back to the 1970s.

    As a child, I learned the importance of color and symmetry as it related to the Christmas trees. These lessons were unique to our household and were offered to me free of charge by John Bell Jr., father, and artist. This story about the Christmas Tree is now one of my favorite memories of Christmas, growing up in the John Bell Jr. household.

    An eddy of dry leaves blew in and danced down through the tile hallway of the dormitory as I peeked out to the back parking lot. I was anxious, waiting for Dad to pick me up to go home from college for the weekend. The semester was winding down and I found myself without a vehicle. Being sequestered on the campus of Arkansas Tech University at Russellville without a vehicle was not a fun experience. Feeling the squeeze between a crushing semester and upcoming finals week, I called home and begged Dad to find someone to come and get me for the weekend. He agreed to come himself. It was 1987, and I was fortunate that Dad was still able to drive. It was noon. He was late.

    Soon I saw the old blue van roll up in the parking lot. I was excited to have Dad see my dormitory Christmas decorations, and excited to go home. Dad let down the wheelchair lift and came to the back door. His hair blew in the wind as I let him in. I shouted out the required, "Man in the hallway!" in case there were any other ladies unfortunate enough to still be there. The dorm was not coed, and this was the antiquated protocol for Massey Hall.

"Dad, you need to come in and see our decorations!" I knew he would be underwhelmed. My roommate and I had found a small Christmas tree at a yard sale. It was decorated with a couple of red Christmas balls, aluminum icicles, and a garland made from the old-style computer printer tractor feed holes. The tree stood atop a small refrigerator. "Dad, check out our tree! What do you think?" I waited.

"Well, your tree looks like it is made of bottle brushes, but aside from that it looks pretty good." He was more complimentary than I thought he would be. He said, "We have a tree at home, and your mother wants to go ahead and decorate it tonight." This was great news. I loved the Bell household tree-decorating tradition.

Feltner's Whatta-Burger in Russellville made the best cheeseburger in the State, hands down. My dormitory on campus was even within view of the place. Dad and I crossed "O" street to visit the establishment before heading home.

Dad drove the big blue van using a wheelchair lift and hand controls allowing him to operate the gas and brake with his hands. This arrangement was something I was used to and gave no thought to. Now I know many people would be reluctant to ride with someone who needed that kind of adaptive equipment to drive. We spent the hour and a half talking about the upcoming holiday and family.

When we pulled up in the drive, Dad said, "Now, your mother made dinner. We won't tell her about the burgers. Put this stuff in the trash can." Dutifully, I deposited shake cups in the outside trash can. He opened the van door, drove his wheelchair out onto the lift, let it down and we both went up the back ramp into the house.

Everything smelled like baked chicken and evergreen It was intoxicating. We lived in a white frame house built in the 1930s. The older homes offered wider doorways and larger rooms than the typical new construction. That construction allowed for better access by wheelchair to the inside spaces. Dad had bought a Christmas tree from the Optimist Club tree lot. He made a deal for them to deliver it to the house and set it up in the stand with a little water in the bottom to keep the tree fresh. I immediately went to check out the tree. It was beautiful, especially compared to my 'bottle brush' tree in the dorm. I could already see the image of the tree reflected in the hardwood floor along with the fire from the fireplace.

I retrieved boxes of decorations from the attic and started unpacking lights and ornaments. Dad's spot in the living room afforded him access to a table with remotes for the television and stereo. He assumed his place and turned the stereo on to play Christmas music. Mom's favorite was Elvis Presley's album called "White Christmas." I grabbed the lights and headed toward the tree. Dad said, "Wait! We need to look at this tree first." I had forgotten the most important part of this operation. Strategy. One had to determine the best side of the tree to face the room. Then the cord to the lights was strategically placed in the tree to reach the outlet. This is not something that needs consideration when you use an artificial tree because all of the sides of the tree are the same. Once the correct side was identified, I grabbed the lights again and headed to the tree.

Dad said, "Wait. Are those lights set to stay on or flash?" Of course, I needed to plug in the lights and look to be sure. The John Bell Jr. tree decoration procedure required that blinking lights be placed on the tree first and needed to be in the middle near the trunk. Then the steady lights were placed toward the outside of the branches. This arrangement allowed some lights to always remain on, while the inside lights blink.

Once the lights were installed, the important homemade decorations were strategically placed on the tree, with some in the middle near the tree trunk. The blinking lights draw the eye to those decorations in the hollows of the tree. One important decoration is a small stocking with "Lisa" stitched on. Mother told me that was made for me by a friend of hers when I was a baby. Mother and I placed the decorations on the tree with direction from Dad. Then the colored balls were the next layer of decoration. These provided a layer of texture to the tree, according to Dad the tree decorator. These were separated around the tree by color to prevent two of the same color from being next to each other. This process sounds tedious, but it was fun to drink eggnog and to hold up a Christmas ball against the tree and have Dad say, "Right, right, now left a little…"

The last step was to add a garland, which lay on top of everything and provided a finish to the tree. This night we made a string of popcorn with cranberries to use for a garland. Mother made some popcorn, plain for the tree and some with salt and butter for us to eat. This particular year we sat eating and stringing popcorn until about midnight. Then the strings went on the tree carefully, so the garland was symmetrical. When the tree was decorated, it was inspected by all and adjusted. Then it was declared finished and complete for the year 1987.

This memory is of a moment in time taken for granted. Now that both John Bell Jr. and Maxie have passed away, this memory is much sweeter to me and brings comfort while I decorate my Christmas tree every year. I have most of those old decorations, and each one speaks to my heart of special times with my parents. Added to the small stocking with "Lisa" stitched on, my tree has one with "Jessie" stitched on for my daughter. One day, there may be another tiny stocking on the tree, adding even more memories.

"The John Bell Jr. tree decoration procedures required that the blinking lights be placed on the tree first and needed to be in the middle near the trunk."

31 🔔 Cabin on the Lake

NESTLED AWAY FROM THE OTHER cabins, the "Cabin on the Lake" at Greenleaf State Park in Oklahoma was our secret family getaway. John Bell Jr. discovered this cabin while working with the Arkansas State Parks on park accessibility for the handicapped. Built in the 1990s with funding from the Southwestern Bell Telephone Pioneers, the two-room cabin boasts complete accessibility, including an accessible fishing pier. Our family reserved it as often as possible.

John and Maxine Bell at Greenleaf State Park "Cabin on the Lake" 2013

Many of our family vacation memories were made there. One of Dad's favorite pastimes was sitting on the screened-in porch and looking out over the lake, drinking a glass of iced tea.

During one of our visits to the Cabin, I remember sitting on the screened-in porch, listening to the cicadas sing. Lake water lapped at the cypress trees shading the little cabin. The early September air was beginning to cool down for the evening. The cabin door was open, and the smell of home cooking floated out, making my stomach growl. I could hear Mother in the kitchen banging pans. The breeze and the smell of cooking made the place feel like home.

Dad was in the living room with his granddaughter, Jessie. She played on a quilt laid out on the floor. Just when we thought Jessie would learn to crawl, she learned how to turn sideways and roll. This development was a large point of discussion among her grandparents, particularly because Jessie was the only grandchild on both sides. She was also beginning to talk, and she had a lot to say to her grandpa.

I heard her little voice say, "Gampa toy!"

Then I heard his wheelchair move. He said, "Where's your toy?"

Later, again Jessie said, "TOY!"

I heard Dad's wheelchair move, and then he said, "Come get your toy."

Curiosity finally got the better of me. Leaving my spot on the porch swing, I leaned in the doorway to peek at what was going on.

On the front of the footrests of Dad's wheelchair were little wheels to protect the walls. Jessie was having a great time on the floor reaching those wheels and making them spin. Once she was getting entertained, Dad would move his wheelchair backwards just a little, and Jessie would crawl a little to reach the wheels again. He gradually backed up farther and farther until she was crawling a long distance across the floor. Jessie's newly developed skill was very exciting to me as a first-and-only-time Mom. I alerted everyone who would listen that dad taught Jessie to crawl. Of course, later I found out that she could get into more trouble than before because she was more mobile.

32 🔔 Birthday Cake Artwork

DECEMBER 1998 WAS THE THIRD birthday of Jessie Shambarger. Jessie was the only granddaughter of John Bell Jr. I purchased a mermaid birthday cake pan complete with some food grade dye for icing. This mermaid and her entourage dominated our household. Even the cat knew all the mermaid songs. The day prior to the epic three-year-old birthday party, I took off the afternoon to bake and decorate the cake.

    With the cake baked and cooled, the decorating part began with mixing up the icing. The kit included a plastic mermaid face which was to put on the cake. This meant that I had to match the face color on the plastic face with the icing color to make her mermaid arms. Mixing the red coloring into the white icing, I had made something that looked like a soft pink color that might go on a nursery wall. I looked at the remaining blue, green, and yellow dye colors and hit a roadblock. Mermaid cake terror welled up in my whole body. If I added blue, I would have a purple Mermaid. I thought I had no time to have someone else make a cake. Just when full panic was rising, I realized I had a great lifeline to color mixing. Dad. "Can he tell me how to make flesh colored icing over the phone?" I did not have the benefit of facetime back then. My only resource was an expensive long distance phone call to a landline. Still, I thought, "Sure he can help me, Dad can do almost anything." I rang the phone in his home studio.

    My heart sank when I heard his recorded voice on the message machine. "Dad! It's Lisa, calling on the bat phone. Call me back!"

    The bat phone was code that meant something was wrong, and help was needed. Batman was one of Dad's favorite characters.

    Luckily, Dad called right back. "What's going on?"

    I told him about the cake predicament. I said I did not want a purple mermaid, and I didn't have any flesh-colored dye. "Dad, I don't have time to get someone else to make a cake! I still have to make snacks for the party."

He could hear the panic in my voice. "Okay, calm down, take a breath," he said. "Here's what you're going to do. What color do you have now?"

I told him, "I have baby girl pink."

He told me to put down the phone and get a saucer and some toothpicks. I got the necessary tools and got back on the phone.

"Okay, I got the stuff," I said.

Then he told me to do something that would strike fear in the heart of any mermaid cake making Mom. He said, "Put one single drop of yellow in the icing and mix it up. Put a drop of blue on your saucer."

"Okay…" I summoned all my blind trust and dropped in the yellow. I mixed and mixed and a flesh color emerged that was pretty close to the mermaid face piece. "Dad!" I said, "It looks great! It's almost a match!" I was elated.

"Now dip your toothpick in the blue and put a tiny bit in the icing. Mix it up good. Do that until the color matches." He said. Then he said, "I gotta go, I have work to do." The line went dead.

The mermaid cake was an amateur job, but she looked pretty good. I put the cake in a bakery box and closed the lid.

Saturday afternoon was party time. Around noon, I saw my parents' red van roll up into the driveway. John and Maxine Bell did not let a two-hour drive stop them from attending the party. Finally cake time came. All of the three-year-old friends, moms and all of the grandparents and Jessie's Dad were around the table. I placed three candles on the cake. Jessie's Dad turned down the lights and I put the cake on the table.

Immediately Jessie yelled out, "Yay it's Ariel!" Relief came over me that she recognized the character. At the other end of the table, I looked at Dad. He winked. I owed this large victory entirely to Dad.

"Just when full panic was rising, I realized I had a great lifeline to color mixing."

33 ♎ The Starship

SITTING IN THE BACK OF my parents' big GMC Savanna van, I buckled on a seat belt for Jessie.

Then sounded the "Ready captain..."

The van didn't move. I looked past dad's wheelchair, which was held in place by a clamp that bolted to the floor and saw Mom in the driver's position, through the rearview mirror looking back at me. She knew I wasn't buckled in. I leaned down and squeezed my arm through the crack in the bench seat where the clip end of my buckle always hid. I hated that seat belt. It hated me too. I searched around on the floor of the van. My hand found something that might be a fire extinguisher... then finally the buckle. I managed to buckle the belt while wondering why there would be a fire extinguisher in the van.

"Ready Captain." I said again. Mom put the big van in gear and backed it out of the garage.

I'm not sure when we started this, but the "Captain" was a thin reference to the Captain on the Star Trek series. To say Dad was a sci fi fan would be an understatement. He enjoyed all the sci fi movies. To watch one of those movies with him resulted in an education about the movie and all the scientific theories behind it.

I thought about this while Mom drove us through the rolling hills of eastern Oklahoma on the way to the family reunion. The mechanics involved in enabling two people in wheelchairs to get in a big van and head down the road would remind a person of a star ship. This was a fact that, on most days, I never thought about because I was so accustomed to travelling this way.

The operation was comprised of several mechanical elements which had to work together. Mom had a small remote that allowed her to open the side doors on the van, to fold out the hydraulic wheelchair lift, and then to lower it to the ground. She then drove her wheelchair onto the lift and used buttons on the lift to raise it to the level of the van floor. Then she drove her wheelchair over to the driver's spot. She used a switch on the van to close a floor mounted clamp onto her chair. Then she used buttons mounted next to her to lower the lift again for Dad to get on. Once this whole operation was completed and he was in place, she closed the van doors and drove using hand controls to operate the gas and the brake. The steering operated with a power assist. All this extra equipment operated using an extra battery mounted under the van.

All that was on my mind this hot summer day as we rolled up to the IGA grocery in the small town of Vain, Oklahoma. As was tradition, we paraded through the little store and bought every unhealthy snack item known to man. We bought enough junk food for an army, all for a weekend trip. While I was unbuckling me and my daughter Jessie, I looked out the window of the van. A lady stood on the sidewalk with a bunch of children. When the van doors opened, and the lift started to fold out, she hoarded her kids behind her with protective arms. She didn't just go on to her car with them because she was too curious to mind her own business.

Dad went out first, and I wasn't sure how he was going to handle this crowd of onlookers. He rolled in his wheelchair out on the lift and looked over at them.

They were half cowering at this sight when he said, "Take me to your leader!"

Lillian Sweeten Bell with John Bell Jr. 2011

Dad was saying, "Turn right, Mom! No! Your other right!"

34 ⌂ Grandma's Pickles

ONE CRISP FALL EVENING JESSIE and I rolled up to the Maxine and John Bell Jr. residence for a weekend visit. We drove a black Nissan 280Z convertible. I had acquired the car second hand, and under the terms of the "Uncle Bill Deal." One lesson I learned from the convertible is that the air temperature is very cold in the Fall at seventy miles per hour. Our hair was blown and lips slightly blue when I put the car in park. Looking forward to my parent's fireplace and a cup of coffee, I climbed out of the car.

The garage door went up, and the GMC Savannah backed out. Jessie and I stood there on the driveway puzzled. Mom and Dad knew we were coming, so where were they going? The van stopped in the driveway and the side doors opened. The wheelchair lift folded out.

Dad came to the door and said, "We have to take the old people and the crippled people to the grocery store." He had a sense of humor about everything.

That explained it. Dad's sister Carolyn developed multiple sclerosis, and now she used a wheelchair too. She was widowed and lived in a small apartment not far from my parents' house. Mom and Dad spent years with no transportation. They knew very well what it was like to need groceries and have no way to go get them. Taking Carolyn and Grandma to the grocery store became a regular occurrence. Fitting three wheelchairs in that van was a feat of engineering. Mom sat in the driver's spot. Dad scooted his wheelchair as far up as he could, and Carolyn squeezed in behind their wheelchairs. Grandma, of course, sat in the passenger seat and supervised everything. Rather than try to cram myself and Jessie into the van with all the old and crippled folks, I decided to meet them at the grocery store.

Standing in the parking lot of the Winton's IGA, we all watched as Dad gave detailed instructions to my 80-year-old

Grandmother on how to drive a battery-operated shopping cart. Grandma drove the cart in circles in the parking lot. The full moon made a glint of light on the basket as Grandma turned circles.

Dad was saying, "Turn right Mom! No, your other right!"

I was thinking, "Now this is something you don't see every day."

That woman had never driven a car, but she seemed to be getting the hang of the cart. My father was extremely good at giving detailed instructions to anyone on how to do just about anything.

The grocery store door boasted a large sign that said, "IN." The automatic door swung open to the wheelchair brigade. Winton's was an old store and always smelled a little musty. Jessie loved her great grandmother, so she volunteered for Great Grandma Detail. I watched as the two headed down the aisle passing the paper towels. Jessie skipped alongside the electric cart. The cart made a high pitched "rrrrrrrr" sound that reminded me of the sound a microwave oven makes set to medium.

Although I wheeled a regular shopping cart, Mom grabbed a hand-held basket and carried it in her lap. I helped Carolyn shop, and we segregated her items from the food I was buying for myself. We all went in a parade of wheelchairs along the meat case. I could hear Jessie and Grandma Bell a couple of isles over. Their little cart went, "rrrrrrrr...." And then, "Beep! Beep! Beep!"

Dad and I had an unwritten, unspoken rule. When in the grocery store, we would split off from everyone and go examine the ice cream so dad could pick out something. Mom and Aunt Carolyn were discussing a pot roast when I saw Dad motion toward the end of the isle. I turned the cart and wheeled after Dad. He led to the Ice cream isle. Rows and rows of multiple colored ice cream tubs seemed to stretch out forever. I could hear Grandma and Jessie one isle over. Dad finally selected his favorite version of butter pecan ice cream, as usual.

I stood holding the Blue Bell when it happened. We heard, "Rrrrrrr....Beep! Beep! CRASH!"

Jessie screamed.

I heard Dad say, "Oh No."

I dropped the ice cream into it and abandoned the cart. Running, I slid around the corner to the next isle.

There was Grandma, her cart underneath a giant pile of pickle jars. Jessie stood nearby. Glass and pickles were all over and a lake of pickle juice was beginning to form on Isle 12. Store employees came running and carefully extracted Grandma from underneath the pickles.

Dad asked her, "How could you have done this? Driving that cart is so easy!"

Grandma said, "I thought it was the brakes…" She stood there wringing her hands while the pickle juice was mopped up. It broke my heart to see her look so worried. She offered to pay for the pickles. The store manager said nobody had to pay for the pickles. There were unbelievably few jars broken. The manager was just glad nobody was hurt. It was probably a bonus that my parents had shopped in that store forever and knew the manager well. We all left the store with our various grocery orders. Forever after, Grandma was banned from driving the battery-operated cart.

35 🔔 Thrift Store Artwork

IT WAS A FRIDAY AFTERNOON, and I was scouring the shelves of my favorite thrift shop looking for a stray John Bell Jr. print someone may have donated. Then I saw it. Stashed behind a velvet poster of dogs playing cards was something with blue sky and a ship mast. I knew it was no John Bell, but still I pulled it out. It was a canvas reproduction of a watercolor, depicting sailboats on water with a city around the water bank. I had just repainted my house inside, and I could see a spot for this artwork. On the back was a tag that said, "blue boats $10." Feeling like a cheater, I snatched it up. It had a blue tag on it, so I got it for only $8. I loaded it in the Prius and took it home.

The painting was propped against the couch when Jessie came home from school. Although I played it down, I was anxiously waiting to hear what she would say about it. I didn't have to wait long to see her standing there looking it over, hands on her hips. I joined her. We looked at the painting for a while.

Finally, she said, "Where did you get this?"

"At my thrift shop," I said, thinking she already knew. "I'm taking it to Fort Smith to show Dad."

"Really, you're going to show him this?"

"Yes, I want to get his opinion about it. What do you think he'll say?"

"Nothing good," she said.

We loaded the painting into the car with our suitcases and rolled out of town on the way to Fort Smith to visit mom and dad.

Early the next day, I padded in my sock feet into the room that served as dad's art studio. The morning sun shone through the windows. Bars of light were cast onto dad's easel holding his painting, 'Cabin on the Lake' in progress. My 'blue boats" was propped against dad's flat files. Admiring his painting, I thought about how silly I felt about showing my 'blue boats' painting to Dad. For a minute, I thought about putting it back in the car.

Later that morning, I saw dad looking intensely at my thrift store painting. A frown was on his face, his eyebrows were lowered.

I said, "So, I picked this up yesterday and thought I'd see what you could tell me about it."

His frown deepened. "What did you pay for this?" he asked.

"Not much." I said, "I like the boats."

Regarding his beautiful 'Cabin on the Lake,' I felt silly.

"What you have here is a sweat shop piece."

Now this sounded intriguing. "Sweat shop?"

"Let me tell you a little about the world of artwork," he said.

I sat down.

"How much did you give for this?"

"I didn't take out a second mortgage...," I said.

"Well, this is not artwork."

I was not surprised to hear him say that. "What is it?"

"Pieces like this are created on an assembly line," he explained. "Someone takes the canvas and paints it blue. Then they pass it down and paint blue on another canvas. Someone else then paints boats, and someone else paints water. At the end you have this painting. They are mass-produced. That's not how real artwork is created."

"It looks like artwork," I said.

He went on to say that a person's ability to paint a canvas blue doesn't make them an artist.

"The value in a piece of artwork," he said, "...lies in the overall artistic talent of the artist as demonstrated in his execution of the whole piece. The value is also in the originality of the piece. You can't create a whole bunch of original paintings that look the same and expect them to have any value."

He went on, "A piece of artwork stands on its own. You also don't create an original painting and then offer the buyer the opportunity to have you overlay the piece with extra paint, thus altering it to 'match their colors.' Those practices make the original lose value."

I looked again at my "blue boats" and I could see his point.

Then he said, "Pieces like this one are mass-produced and sold cheap. Sometimes they make several similar ones with different colors so you can pick one to match your color scheme. But these pieces have no real value."

Again, he looked at me and seemed to study my face.

"Eight dollars," I said.

Dad shook his head.

"Do you think David Gates would frame it for me?" I asked.

"Yes," he said.

And so, it was.

36 ♝ Avatar

TO BE PART OF THE John Bell Jr. family was to understand his intense appreciation for sci fi movies. He donned the heavy framed 3-D glasses with glee. Readily, he was transported into the scene masterfully created by Stephen Spielberg. Bathed in deep blues and greens, John moved freely through jungle terrain. This immersion was made more intense by the 5-point surround system installed in his living room. His 47-inch-high-definition television was perched on a table. It had been custom made to the right height to allow viewing at the best optical level. Spread across the small table he used in the living room were several remote controls. This arrangement was what I called dad's "Command Control Center." Under no circumstances did anyone place any object on his table to block any controller signal. Neither did anyone move or touch anything on his table.

    David Gates worked with John for several years in a partnership arrangement which enabled David to frame and assist in selling work. This partnership meant the world to John, allowing David to be the "front of the house" for his work. It is safe to say that David Gates knew John Bell Jr. better than many.

    When I talked to David Gates about John and his love of movies, he explained, "John had an appreciation for the artistic side of the movies, but for him they were also an escape. The one thing he wanted more than anything was to be like everyone else. The thought that there might be an Avatar that he could create enthralled him. Imagine the freedom he would feel if he were able to step outside of the body he was trapped in with so many physical limitations! He loved to imagine that scenario, to be free to be anything he wanted to be."

John Bell Jr. and David Gates 2002

37 ♗ The Mysterious Lady

JOHN BELL JR. WAS VERY organized and meticulous in his work. The discovery of the mysterious lady, buried in the bottom drawer of his flat files was perplexing. The image of the lady, reposed on a bed wearing only a sheer covering, floated on the page. It was a watercolor. Mom and I studied the image. The style was unusual for a John Bell, as the paper around her image was bare. So was the Lady. She wore only a smile.

"Is this finished or is it just a sketch he made?" I asked Mom.
"I'm not sure…," she said.
"Who is this?"
Mom said, "I'm not sure of that either."

The discovery of this painting was made after John Bell Jr. passed away, leaving us to guess about this painting. Based on the signature at that bottom, we decided it was finished. The style of the piece and the signature seemed to indicate it was done around 1974.

Then the search for the identity of the damsel was on. Mother contacted everyone she thought would have any information about her. Nobody knew her. Is she just someone who was made up in the mind of John Bell Jr? Is she someone he knew?

The painting of the Mysterious Lady was displayed at the Regional Art Museum art show in October 2017. When it was time for the artwork to come back home from the Museum, Mom was not interested in the Lady returning. She wanted to be the only woman of the house. The lady came home with me, as I feared for her future, being so vulnerable and unclad. The identity of the Lady remains a mystery. Now the Mysterious Lady resides in the hands of the Fort Smith Regional Art Museum. The residence of the Lady there allows everyone who sees her to guess her identity.

"The sunrise of a new day shone in my window with striking bright yellow sunshine and a sky dotted with pink and blue clouds."

38 ♫ Passing of the Torch

OF ONE THING, I WAS sure. It was the middle of the night. Something woke me from a sound sleep. I opened my eyes to almost complete darkness. Almost dark. A dim light emanated from my phone. I bounced out of bed to my feet, reaching for it. I heard a crash as my lamp landed in the floor. The little screen read: Friday, November 8: '04:57' and "MOM." I knew what had happened. My knees got weak. I collapsed to the floor with my back against the bed, my feet near the fallen lamp.

"Hello Mom?" I croaked into the phone. I could hear it in her voice. Mom had been crying.

"Lisa, He's GONE."

The only thing I could get out was, "Oh NO!"

Mom said. "Oh Lisa! We should have sent him to the hospital last night. I knew we should have sent him! He might still be here!"

My mind reeled. I had to help her, but I was two hours away. While fighting to control my emotions, I remembered our conversation from the previous night.

"Mom?"

She was crying.

"We talked about Dad last night," I said. "Remember what he said to you about the hospital? You told me he adamantly refused to go. You said he looked tired, and that you knew he just wanted to rest."

In that conversation, Mom told me that Dad was very sick. Diagnosed with cancer in August, he had just completed his last round of chemotherapy. Our good friend Cornell came to help Dad to bed. Once he was settled, Mom talked to Dad about how sick he was. She pleaded with him to let her call the paramedics to take him to the hospital.

She told me he had said, "NO! Don't do that."

Now, about six hours later, I said, "Mom, we decided together last night to let him rest and to see how he was doing in the morning."

Mom said, "I KNEW we should have sent him…"

"If we had sent him to the hospital, Dad would have passed away in a hospital with people poking him every thirty minutes. This way he was able to go home to the Lord while asleep in his own bed."

All I heard was her crying. I longed to be there now. The image of my mom, all alone, was heartbreaking.

She finally broke the silence. "I need to get off here and call the coroner."

I said, "Wait Mom, let me call Uncle Jim and Cornell. I'll get them to come over. Then I'll get Jessie up and we'll get on the road." We agreed, and the line went dead.

The darkness closed in around me again. I was alone in my room, sitting on the floor. The little phone screen said, '05:42' when I rang Uncle Jim. Dad's brother, Jim, was ten years younger than him. A retired Fire Marshall, Jim had rescued my family many times over the years. I felt numb. The impact of Dad's death had not fully registered until I heard Uncle Jim's voice. He must have thought I had lost my mind. He was right.

It all came out at once. "Uncle Jim, Dad passed away. He died, and Mom is all alone at the house. She's calling the coroner. Can you go help her?"

I only remember him saying, "What?" and then, "Yes I'm on my way over there."

Cornell was my next call. When he answered, I was struggling to keep control of my voice. I told him Dad had passed away.

He said, "John Bell? John has passed?"

I knew it was impossible to believe. "Yes." There was silence. "I need to get Jessie packed up and call work." I told him I would be there as soon as I could get there. I was two hours away.

"You take care of you and Jessie. I'll go help your mom."

I got myself up from the floor and went into the kitchen. The sunrise of a new day shone in my window with striking bright yellow sunshine and a sky dotted with pink and blue clouds. It felt surreal.

"How could the sun rise so beautifully on this, the first daybreak on a world without my dad in it?" As I stood there, tears came.

Time to adjust was not a luxury I could afford. Calls needed to be made and suitcases packed. Tina Bright has known me and my family since we were both in high school. Time apart nor the three-hour distance between us made any difference. She is always my first call when I need help. It was comforting to hear her voice.

She asked, "Are you okay?"

"No. No I'm not."

"Is there anyone who can drive you to Fort Smith?"

"No." I said, "Jessie can drive but she's not in any shape. I need to pack but Jessie is crying and not packing her things. I don't know what to do."

Tina was off work that day. She said, "I'll go help your mom. Just get out a suitcase and pack Jessie's things and put her in the car."

I will forever be indebted to Tina for her help that day.

The familiar highway unfolded in front of us as Jessie and I drove in silence. At about the halfway point, my phone rang.

Tina said, "Oh I was just wondering how far out you are."

I could tell by her voice that something was going on at the house. "We're about 45 minutes out. Is Mom, okay?"

She assured me Mom was as good as possible, and just wanted a time frame for the funeral home. Knowing something was going down at the house, I put the hammer down.

Finally, the old frame house was in view. Cars were everywhere. I squeezed my Prius into a spot in front of the house and hurried to the front door. The house was packed with people. Phones were ringing. Mom came and hugged me amid the chaos, and everything stopped for a minute.

"Oh Honey," she said. "Are you okay?" It struck me that she was thinking of me when she had just lost her husband of 50 years.

Tina held a yellow pad of paper full of names and numbers. She had been running a communications station from the house.

She told me, "I've been telling people 'Yes Mr. Bell has passed away', and 'I don't have any more information right now.'"

Then she said, "Three television stations have called wanting an interview."

It seemed absurd that such a personal loss to my family would be a public affair. After all, we were not celebrities.

I said, "What? We're not doing any television interviews."

Tina said, "You had better talk to your mom about that."

Mom felt like the people of the City of Fort Smith had been so good to our family throughout Dad's career that they deserved a television interview to inform them of his passing. We talked about how hard it would be to do an interview for a television station since we were all grieving. She said, "I know it'll be hard. I can do it though. Fort Smith deserves at least that." She picked the station, and we set up a time with them.

Amidst the swirl of people coming and going and phones ringing, three people came in with television equipment. They set up in Dad's art studio. Tina and I sat on each side of the camera person, and they started rolling film. Bathed in bright lights, Mom looked small and vulnerable in front of the camera. The reporter asked a million questions.

Then finally he asked, "What did it feel like when you went to his side and tried to wake him this morning?" I was too far away. I looked at Tina.

Tina stepped in front of the camera and said, "This interview is over."

The days that followed were packed. A fulltime coordinator wrangled phone calls, visitors, and parking. My friend Willard Wentz served as casserole deflector. Neighbors hid in their houses when we came to their door with rolls and chicken spaghetti.

Although Dad had wanted cremation, Mom felt strongly that the people of Fort Smith needed to see him at the funeral service so they could say goodbye. Ocker-Putman Funeral Home came across the caller identification on Mom's landline, and she rushed to answer.

I was getting dressed when Mom hurried in saying, "They have your dad ready!"

I wondered what that meant. We rolled up to the front door of the funeral home in Mom's GMC Savana van just like we owned the place. I watched as Mom unlocked her wheelchair, opened the van door, and let the wheelchair lift down.

While Mom was in a hurry, I was not in a hurry to see my father lying in a casket. The Funeral Director opened the big wooden doors and invited us into the great foyer. The furnishings were beautiful. Plush stuffed couches, polished wooden tables with vases of flowers adorned the whole facility. It smelled like a flower shop. Mom stopped to examine an arrangement of white and blue flowers on the way in.

She exclaimed, "Oh these are from David and Shirley! They are beautiful."

It was then that I realized all those flowers were sent to our family as condolences. They were not flowers provided by the funeral home to make things look pretty. The magnitude of the outreach and support from family and friends warmed my heart.

Mom headed into the chapel area with the Funeral Director in tow. I followed behind. I could see an open casket in the front of the chapel. The only thing making it possible for me to walk up to that casket was the thought that my mother might have to view her husband of 50 years in a coffin without me by her side. I stood next to her as she reached in and touched his hand. Dad was dressed in a tan plaid shirt and trousers just as he would be if he were working in his art studio. He bore a great resemblance to the large photo of John Bell Jr. which stood nearby on an easel. It seemed odd that I would compare his body with the photo of him, but this body did not seem to be Dad at all. Mom and the Funeral Director discussed Dad's appearance, and it was decided that he looked just fine. Everything was ready for the family visitation.

When we were ready to leave, I asked to have a few minutes alone with Dad. I could hear Mom and Jessie talking as they walked down the aisle of the chapel to the foyer. I stood next to the casket looking at him. The big doors out front closed. The place was quiet. I considered Dad's hands, folded across his torso. I thought about all that he had done with those hands for seventy-six years. I considered his artwork and family picnics holding hamburgers. I considered his eyes, at rest now. He had a way of viewing the world that most people can't see.

When it seemed that I would never be able to leave his side, Dad's words came to me almost like he was there speaking. He was always able to take a bad situation and to put a positive spin on it.

On the subject of Death, Funerals and Coffins, Dad would say, "When somebody is dead, they always say, 'Oh he looks so good!' I say NO. He doesn't look good. He's DEAD. He looks DEAD!"

His words echoed in my mind. A quiet peacefulness settled over me. Before I walked away, I said out loud, "No Dad, you really do look good. I know you are dead and not here at all. But you do look good. For a dead person."

I knew if he could hear my words, he would understand.

39 🔔 The Woman Behind the Man

IF ANYTHING AT ALL IS clear, it is the undeniable fact that Maxine was the woman behind the man who was John Bell Jr. Without her unwavering support, none of his success would have been possible. My earliest memories are of Mom getting up early in the morning to make his lunch. Many mornings I awoke to the sound of Mother breaking ice cubes to fit in Dad's Stanley thermos for his iced tea.

Maxine was a true-to-life homemaker, raising me and supporting us all with meals and mended clothes. Although Maxine also used a wheelchair, her limitations did not stop her from achieving her goals, or from helping John achieve his.

Later in life, when John became unable to drive, she took the wheel. Many roads saw a full-size van rolling with Maxine at the wheel and John right beside her. When the window was down, the roadside critters heard John trying to tell her how to drive.

When I went to college, Maxine went to work to help support our family. She worked for the Fort Smith Community Clearinghouse for several years handing out food boxes to needy people. She also worked for the Literacy Council of Western Arkansas, coordinating the English as a Second Language program.

As John aged, he lost flexibility and with it, the ability to do lots of things for himself. Maxine filled in for him and took care of whatever was required for him to be able to work and live a full life. When I was grown, my room in their home was adjacent to Dad's home art studio. It was common to overhear their discussions about which paint he needed for the day. I can still hear two wheelchairs maneuvering in the studio while Maxine squeezed out paint on a pallet. In my memory, I can still smell the turpentine.

As he aged, it became difficult for John to feed himself. John was a very proud man and concerned about how he was perceived. He was more worried about spilling food on himself than he was about people seeing Maxine helping him eat. Many a Fort Smith restaurant saw the two eating. Maxine would eat her meal while alternately allowing him to choose what food went on his fork.

All this time John continued to produce beautiful paintings. Those who saw the two in restaurants likely never imagined that, before them, and being assisted by his wife, they would see the legendary artist. During his last days, Maxine consoled him as they both watched his abilities, his very life, slip away. She was by his side when he took his last breath. Following his death, Maxine championed his life while taking no credit for her supporting role. Indeed, they were a team. One could not exist without the other.

Acknowledgements

The tales told in this book seemed to live and breathe when recounted by John Bell Jr. in person. Capturing the spirit of those tales in a book is a difficult task. The conception of this project happened years ago. John Bell Jr. sat telling the stories of his life around the holiday dinner table. All agreed that "We have got to write these stories in a book." There are many more stories to tell which lie in the hearts and minds of those people who knew John Bell Jr.

Special thanks go to the many family members and friends who took time to speak to me for hours, sometimes over bad phone connections, recounting memories of John Bell Jr. The overwhelming eagerness of contributors and the feeling of love for John has been heartwarming. Those people include Jim and Sharron Bell, Michael Calicott, Clifton Culpepper, Harry Elledge, David Gates, Jason Gilkey, Perry Grizzle, Bill Kropp III, Bradley Martin, and Alison Thieben. Thank you to the family and friends mentioned in the book.

Thank you to Alison Thieben for helping with the story content, and to Bill Kropp II for contributing the book title. The more the book took shape, the more I was convinced that the title was indeed the spirit of it. Many thanks to Julie Moncrief for editing and design ideas. Thank you to Tina and Keith Bright at Home Video Studio for photo editing. I am forever grateful for the endless patience of my husband DeWayne Wilson concerning my many hours of book writing.

Many thanks to the businesses and entities who appear in the book as mentioned in the stories told by John. Thank you to the Arkansas and Oklahoma State Parks, Arkansas Rehabilitation Services, Feltner's Whatta-Burger, Fort Smith Northside High School, the Fort Smith Trolley Museum, Ocker-Putman Funeral Home, the Fort Smith Regional Art Museum, The Literacy Council of Western Arkansas, Sparks Hospital (Now Baptist Hospital), the University of Arkansas, and the Western Arkansas Employment Development Agency.

The bar mentioned in the story about the abandoned building was called "Lakeside," and the drive-in mentioned in the Ford Fairlane story was called "Beverly's."

This book also mentions many family members and friends who have passed away, and who continue to be held dear in our hearts. This was written to honor their memory as well. The lofty hope is this book can bring people together the same way John Bell Jr. did while recounting the tales of his life around the holiday dinner table.

About the Author

Lisa Bell-Wilson is the daughter of John Bell Jr. and wife Maxine. Born in Fayetteville, Arkansas, she was raised in Fort Smith. She followed in her father's footsteps and works with individuals with disabilities providing advocacy and job services. Mrs. Bell-Wilson lives in Conway, Arkansas with her husband DeWayne.

www.ingramcontent.com/pod-product-compliance
Lightning Source LLC
Chambersburg PA
CBHW051131160426
43195CB00014B/2430